Critical analysis skills
for social workers

Critical analysis skills for social workers

David Wilkins and Godfred Boahen

Open University Press

Open University Press
McGraw-Hill Education
McGraw-Hill House
Shoppenhangers Road
Maidenhead
Berkshire
England
SL6 2QL

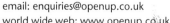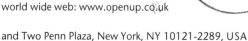

email: enquiries@openup.co.uk
world wide web: www.openup.co.uk

and Two Penn Plaza, New York, NY 10121-2289, USA

First published 2013

Copyright © David Wilkins and Godfred Boahen, 2013

A catalogue record of this book is available from the British Library

ISBN-13: 978-0-33-524649-6 (pb)
ISBN-10: 0-33-524649-4 (pb)
eISBN: 978-0-33-524650-2

Library of Congress Cataloging-in-Publication Data
CIP data applied for

Typesetting and e-book compilations by
RefineCatch Limited, Bungay, Suffolk
Printed and bound by CPI Group (UK) Ltd, Croydon, CR0 4YY

Fictitious names of companies, products, people, characters and/or data that may
be used herein (in case studies or in examples) are not intended to represent any
real individual, company, product or event.

Praise for this book

'Successive reports into social work training, as well as their practice after qualification, identify gaps in professionals' capacity for critical analysis. This excellent book contains thought-provoking examples, each derived from an authentic practice-base and theoretically driven models. Here we have a compelling text which social workers at all stages of their careers should view as essential reading.'

David Shemmings, Visiting Professor of Child Protection Research at Royal Holloway, University of London, UK

'A timely and appropriate post-Munro book for social workers at all levels of experience. The chapter on emotion, intuition and critical analysis is a particularly welcome addition to the subject. A really useful book.'

Dr Jane Reeves, Director of Studies, M.A. Child Protection, Co-Director Centre for Child Protection, University of Kent, UK

'This is a quite splendid book. Sane, fresh, accessible, reader-friendly and a pleasure to read. Taking the meaning skills of critical analysis as the spine of good practice, Wilkins and Boahen have given us a book that succeeds in engaging readers equally at different levels – and one different from anything else on the market.'

Professor Ian Shaw, University of York, UK

Contents

Acknowledgements

We would like to thank the following people for their contributions and their help, without which this book would not have been written: Hayley Wilkins and Jo Longley for their remarkable patience and unwavering support, Janet Wilkins for her thoughtful reading of many draft chapters, Robert Cass for helping to produce the case studies and not least, Katherine Hartle, Alexandra Nowosiad, Rachel Crookes and Alison Davis from McGraw Hill, who guided us through the writing and production process with skill and expertise. Finally, we thank Colin Owens for his editing and Denise Tucker for preparing the index.

Introduction

Analysis is a critical skill for social workers. It is also a skill that many practitioners find very difficult. This assertion is supported by the findings of Serious Case Reviews,[1] inspections and research. Take, for example, Serious Case Reviews, which have consistently identified problems with the quality of analysis in cases where children have died or been seriously injured (see Brandon et al. 2009). Take, as another example, research which finds social workers tend to collect lots and lots of information but without analysing it (e.g. Helm 2011). In Adult services, similar findings have been made. For example, the Executive Summary of a Serious Case Review conducted by Tameside Adult Safeguarding Partnership in 2011 says that 'meetings were held to share information . . . but analysis of the issues . . . [was] sometimes lacking' (p. 48; no special criticism is implied of Tameside, this is just an example of a not uncommon finding).

Why social workers should have difficulty with such a critical skill is a vital question for the profession. This book is not aimed at answering this question per se but at helping social workers improve their analytical skills. We do, however, intend to explore some possible answers to this question here in the Introduction. We do so in order to place this book into context, a context in which we need to acknowledge just why it is that analytical thinking can be so difficult, especially in a field as highly charged, emotionally and intellectually, as social work. Before we do so, we want to ensure that readers are clear about the definition of critical analysis we will be using throughout the book.

Defining critical analysis

You can easily find any number of definitions of analysis via search engines such as Google (other search engines are available, as are actual dictionaries). All of them are fairly similar, defining analysis as a process of detailed examination, aimed at developing a greater understanding of the thing being examined. Some definitions add that by undertaking analysis you will be in a better position to select an appropriate course of action. One can translate this into a three-step process – examining the elements of something; gaining a better understanding of it; and then selecting a course of action. The notion of critical analysis (as opposed to 'just' analysis) is an evolution of this three-step model, highlighting the need to think about and weigh up different elements of information rather than accepting everything at face value. One can see how analysing the results of, say, a scientific experiment in the field of physics would not need to be critical in this way because one is dealing with things like particles. However, in social work, if a parent tells you that their child suffered an injury when they ran into a door, if the child of an older adult tells you their father must be placed into residential care, if the mother of a young man with mental health difficulties tells you he needs stronger medication as she cannot cope – then you cannot simply accept this information uncritically. That is, you need to think critically about why you are being given this information and what it might mean.

How do we think (or, why is analysis so difficult)?

Having provided a definition of critical analysis, we hope the reader will now indulge us for a short time as we explore three possible reasons as to why social workers – and indeed, many people – find critical analysis so difficult. In the reports of Professor Eileen Munro (2010, 2011a, 2011b), and in many other places, various answers are given such as the time pressure that social workers face, the defensiveness of many social work organizations, and so on. Rather than summarize these kinds of findings, useful as they are, we have instead turned to the fields of cognitive psychology and social psychology for a different type of answer.

Mental activity is like physical activity

A moment's reflection on our own lives will make it clear that we make many, many decisions every day and that a majority of these decisions do not feel very much like decisions at all and certainly do not require us to engage in critical, analytical thinking. Common decisions, such as whether to drink tea or coffee, watch TV or listen to the radio, go to the gym or stay at home, do not generally require much thought at all and it can almost feel like we are operating on something akin to an auto-pilot, going about our routines in a similar way from day to day, week to week and month to month.

However, there are other types of decisions that just as clearly require a degree of analysis. Whether to move home, to form a serious, romantic relationship or to have invasive and potentially risky medical treatment are just some of the decisions that people face that require their critical and analytical faculties (or can do). As a result, these kinds of decisions often feel harder to make. So far, so straightforward. But what is less obvious, perhaps, is that mental activity is in many ways similar to physical activity. It is clear from various research studies that the harder you have to think, the more effort it takes and this is more than just a metaphor. Research by Gailliot et al. (2007) shows that strenuous mental activity uses up energy in the form of glucose from the body. Thinking hard – like physical effort – drains your energy reserves and can leave you feeling physically exhausted. From this, it entails that even the *thought* of hard, mental activity can be daunting, in the same way that for most (sensible) people, the thought of running a marathon would be daunting.

Kahneman (2011) discusses an interesting study of judges sitting on a parole board and relates this to the finding that mental activity uses up the body's resources in a similar way to physical activity. The study, by Danziger, Levav and Avnaim-Pesso (2011), found that on average, 35 per cent of parole requests were approved with the remaining 65 per cent declined. A more detailed examination of the rates of approval and decline found that after breaks for food and drink, the rate of approval increased to 65 per cent and fell steadily towards zero until the time of the judges' next break. As Kahneman concludes, the best interpretation of this data is that the judges' decision-making, their analysis of the merits of each request for parole, was affected by their own hunger and fatigue. If you are ever unfortunate enough to find yourself before a parole board, try and make sure your case is discussed straight after lunch.

The similarity between mental and physical activity may go some way to explaining why social workers tend to focus more on gathering information than analysing it. When faced with easier or harder tasks, it can be very tempting to choose the easier one. Given the choice between running or cycling to work, we suspect most people would choose cycling; given the choice between cycling or taking the bus, we suspect most people would choose the bus. Given the choice between running a marathon or not, we know that most people choose not to. The same may well be true for mental activity. Given the choice between gathering information or gathering *and* analysing information, most social workers tend to choose just information gathering.

Telling stories

Although we have argued that people often choose to do easier tasks rather than more difficult ones, it is also the case that people can be motivated to engage in more difficult tasks, even when they do not have to. For example, many people are members of a gym. Some people even make use of their membership to actually go to the gym and work out (it's true). What we want to explore a little here are the stories that people tell themselves. Imagine that you are the member of a gym and an avid exerciser. One evening, you happen to find yourself at home on the sofa rather than down at the gym, pumping iron. We know that people like to make sense of their lives and of the things that happen to them by fitting them into a coherent story or narrative. As a gym-goer who finds herself at home on the sofa, you may well tell yourself (and others) that you remain fully committed to your exercise regime but on this particular evening, your favourite TV programme is on or perhaps you have had an exhausting day at work. However, given that you are a gym-goer, you will definitely be going to the gym tomorrow night and, in all likelihood, you will work out *extra hard* to make up for the evening spent on the sofa.

The recognition that it is not the objective world per se that influences us, so much as our interpretation of it, has been familiar to philosophers and others for centuries. What we now know is that the narratives we construct – the interpretations we place on events – are usually formed quickly and unconsciously (Wilson 2011). While it is possible to consciously challenge these quick-and-easy narratives, this takes mental effort and, as we saw above, mental effort can be just as tiring as physical effort. Another example may help. Imagine you attend a job interview and are not offered the position.

Straightaway – based on your initial, gut reaction – you may feel embarrassed or perhaps angry with yourself or the interview panel. Later on, you might reflect that perhaps the job was not right for you in the first place and you might start to feel quite pleased that you were not offered the position because now, you have the chance to find something really suited to your skills and abilities.

Neither narrative – that you failed nor that you had a lucky escape – can be classified as objectively true but this does not really matter because they are subjective truths only. Of course, whether you could bring yourself to believe in a narrative in which you had a 'lucky escape' would depend on various, complicated factors, including your previous experiences, your sense of self-worth and so on. Depending on these factors, you would need to exert more or less mental effort to construct the 'lucky escape' narrative.

We also know that some narratives are more or less amenable to change than others. So-called core narratives – such as those obtained from early relational experiences – are far more difficult to change than more fleeting narratives, such as those related to a job interview (see Howe et al. 1999, Chapter 2). An understanding of narratives and the importance they play in our experience of events may partly explain the relative popularity of things like posting status updates on social media sites – could this be a way in which people are trying to control their own narratives? Posting an update such as 'Dumped by my boyfriend! Good for me, now I'm free' could be interpreted as a quite obvious way of attempting to consciously control the impact of what might otherwise be an emotionally painful event. Indeed, there is evidence to suggest that consciously writing our own narratives (in the form of a diary entry rather than a status update) can help people process even very traumatic events (such as fire fighters who have seen and rescued injured people from fires; see Pennebaker and Seagal 1999).

One can see how the conscious construction of narratives, which takes mental effort, is going to be susceptible to the tendency people have to choose easier activities over more difficult ones. In other words, people may tend towards the construction of easier, less challenging narratives than the construction of more challenging ones. In social work practice, this often results in a practitioner's first – possibly unconscious – narrative about a service user being difficult to challenge, even when new and contradictory information becomes available. Constructing more nuanced, complex narratives that are open to change based on new information is hard work. This tendency, referred to by Munro (1996, 2008) as confirmation bias, provides another answer to the question of why social workers find critical analysis so difficult.

Making changes

Our third answer to the question of why social workers find critical analysis so difficult is related to the issue of how people make changes. Given that the profession has been aware of the need to improve critical and analytical thinking for many years, one might wonder why inquiry and inspection reports continue to raise it as an issue. In other words, why have we yet to change?

There exists a 'common sense' view that people are largely creatures of habit and generally speaking, do not like change. While this is true up to a point, it is clearly not true in every case. As noted by Heath and Heath (2011), people will make huge changes in their lives, often with at least a modicum of choice, and adapt to them pretty well. If your manager at work asked you to change your duties, to include working longer hours, including at night and weekends, being screamed at, sicked on and for less money, surely every one of us would say 'no'. However, people regularly choose to have babies and most people cope pretty well, most of the time. On the other hand, there are seemingly quite simple changes that people find much more difficult to make, such as giving up smoking. Why should it be the case that some apparently minor changes are so difficult while other major changes are so common?

One explanation is because of the two major systems or 'sides' of the brain involved in making such changes or decisions: the emotional or intuitive side and the rational or conscious side. Haidt (2007) drew a wonderful mental image of the difference between these two systems, which he called the Elephant (the intuitive part) and the Rider (the rational part). The Rider often feels in control but ultimately, if the Elephant decides to take a particular direction, the Elephant will tend to win out, at least for a time. In order for the Rider to 'persuade' the Elephant to change course, the Rider must expend considerable will power, which takes considerable mental effort. Heath and Heath (2011) argue that rather than seeing the Rider as being the brain's strength and the Elephant as the brain's weakness, both parts have weaknesses and strengths. In order to make changes most effectively, you need to engage your Rider and Elephant in the same direction at the same time. Therefore, even if you rationally decide that smoking is bad for you and you want to quit, your Elephant can ensure that you buy another packet of cigarettes and succumb to temptation before the Rider can successfully intervene. Equally, when you intuitively want a child and rationally decide you are ready, the experience can be quite wonderful and for most people, relatively easy to achieve (looking after them for another 18 years and more is another matter!).

We think this links to critical analysis in two ways. First, 'rationally deciding' to be more analytical in your practice is unlikely to be successful if your intuitive side is not on board with the change. Second, there is a link between being able to balance your intuitive and rational responses to service users. When attempting to be more analytical in practice, many social workers may believe, in error, that this means ignoring one's emotional and intuitive responses and relying solely on rationality – the problem, as we have seen, is that the Elephant is not easily ignored, especially in the kind of emotion-ally charged situations that social workers often encounter.

In conclusion, mental activity can be hard work and, like physical exertion, the harder or more complex the mental activity, the more (physical) effort it takes to complete it. Considering the kinds of complex situations that social workers and related professionals often encounter, it is not surprising that they seem to find critical and analytical thinking so difficult. We have examined the tendency people have to create narratives about themselves and others and the power these narratives can have over how you feel and respond to events. We have also seen how difficult it can be to write a new narrative, even when new information becomes available. Finally, we have seen how making changes can be both difficult and relatively easy, depending on one's motivation for it.

We will return to some of these ideas periodically throughout the book and link them further to the practice of critical, analytical social work.

Why we wrote this book

Our main reason for writing this book is because we both believe in the value of social work and because we recognize the range of hugely complex circumstances in which social workers practice. As such, it concerns us that social workers continue to report difficulties in critical analysis. However, as Professor Eileen Munro set out in her review of the child protection and safeguarding systems in England, we do not believe that individual error or poor practice is to blame for this. Rather, the 'system' itself seems almost designed to discourage critical analysis. Munro's recommendations, which are being implemented by the UK Government, are aimed at transforming the child protection system so as to allow more open, reflective and critical practice to flourish. Nevertheless, along with these systemic changes, there are many practitioners – especially those who are not yet qualified or who qualified in the past 10–15 years – whose primary experience of social work will most likely be under the system that Munro has so clearly critiqued (and even if you have worked in fields other than child protection, we think you would recognize much of the practice that Munro critiques from the field of child protection).

We have also become frustrated with the relatively pervasive view that analysis can be thought of as a separate part of practice. For example, *The Framework for the Assessment of Children in Need and their Families* (Department of Health, Department for Education and Employment and Home Office 2000) says that analysis is the final stage of an assessment process. Our view is that practitioners need to develop an 'analytical mindset' that pervades their practice in all areas. In other words, our view is that critical analysis cannot be undertaken as a separate part of social work practice and that you cannot divide your practice into two phases, information gathering and then analysis, despite what the official guidance may say. Indeed, we think it is potentially risky to try to do so.

The Professional Capabilities Framework for social workers in England

Improving analytical skills is also a key part of the new Professional Capabilities Framework (PCF) for social workers, as developed by the Social Work Reform Board in England. Domain 6 of the PCF describes the use of critical analysis in informing and providing reasonable grounds for decisions taken by social workers. We both welcome this new framework, especially the understanding of critical analysis demonstrated in domain 6, which is far more in keeping with our own understanding than that demonstrated in previous guidance, such as *The Framework for the Assessment of Children in Need and Their Families* (discussed above).

The PCF also sets out the progression that social workers are expected to demonstrate as they qualify as social workers and gain more experience. The PCF refers to the different levels that social workers will operate at, from prequalifying (students), to qualified, then experienced and then advanced. We have used a similar approach throughout this book, seeking to demonstrate how practitioners can build on their existing abilities and skills of critical analysis and develop more advanced abilities and skills as their confidence and proficiency increases.

Finally in this section, the new professional registration body for social workers in England, the Health and Care Professions Council, requires registrants to undertake a mixture of continuing professional development activities relevant to current or future practice and we hope that practitioners who read this book will be able to reflect upon their learning and use the practice examples and other learning opportunities as a contribution to their own continuing professional development.

Range and application

We have written this book with any and all social workers in mind. Although social work is a very diverse profession, we do not think that the skills needed to undertake critical analysis will vary significantly from setting to setting or from practitioner to practitioner. We also believe this book could be invaluable for students at the outset of their social work training and for students on placements. We also hope practice assessors will find this book helpful as well as professionals from related or associated fields, such as community nurses, health visitors and teachers (especially those with additional pastoral or child/adult protection responsibilities). We have included practice examples from both children and adult fields of practice and believe that the core skills of critical analysis will be the same for practitioners regardless of background.

Individual practitioners will benefit from working through the book from cover to cover, reading the chapters in order and completing the various tasks and exercises in order to practise and develop their analytical skills and their analytical mindset. However, the book can also be used in other ways. For example, you could use the tools in Chapter 4 in supervision with your line manager; or groups of practitioners could discuss the extended case studies in Chapter 7 as a form of group supervision or development. The same could apply to students at universities or on other types of training courses, for example, using the case studies as part of a seminar discussion.

A word of warning: just reading this book (or any book) will not teach you how to be an analytical thinker. However, by reading this book, practising the necessary skills, using the tools to help you and, perhaps most importantly, valuing the outcome of being more analytical in your practice, we sincerely believe that anyone can do it.

Limitations

The main limitation of this book is that it is focused purely on critical analysis and related skills. Therefore, this book is not about how to gather information, it will not help you understand specific areas such as child development or the psychology of ageing and neither is it particularly focused on decision-making. However, we do feel that this limitation is also the main strength of the book – because social workers are quite frequently criticized for a lack of good quality analysis, it is our view that more should be done to help them develop in this area and we hope our book can contribute.

Layout and learning aids

Each of the chapters will seek to discuss one primary theme or idea and as indicated above, this should help practitioners or students who wish to 'dip into' the book without necessarily reading it from cover to cover. The theme or idea of each chapter is set out in the chapter title and explained in more detail in the introduction. The following features are used throughout the book: chapter overviews, practice examples, research summaries, exercises and reflection points. At the end of each chapter, we have included a summary of the main learning points as well as suggestions for further reading and useful resources.

Chapter summaries

Chapter 1 explores the concept of analysis and why it is such an important skill in practice. We seek to explore what good analysis allows us to do that poor or absent analysis does not. Part of this exploration involves a comparison of analysis with the similar but different concepts of summarizing and decision-making and we also look at how analysis can inform good decision-making and lead to better outcomes for service users.

We also explore different types of thinking, specifically intuitive or emotional compared with rational or conscious. We seek to show how the very best analysis combines elements of both of these two broad categories. We also consider some of the factors that can impact on the process of analytical thought.

Chapter 2 looks at the skills that underpin critical analysis. The skills of time management and planning, critical understanding, logical thinking, research-mindedness, creativity, communication, reflection, hypothesizing and hard work are all explored, with practical examples and tasks to help you assess your own competence and ability in each area, as well as tips and pointers as to how you might improve.

Chapter 3 looks at the important role of emotion and intuition in critical analysis. Initially, this may seem counter-intuitive; after all, isn't critical analysis about reason and rationality and the exclusion of emotional responses? We argue that not only is this unrealistic – how can one reasonably exclude emotional responses in a field such as social work? – but also that it is not conducive to good social work practice.

Chapter 4 considers three models that can aid analysis. We look at each model in turn and demonstrate how they have been applied. We then seek to explore how they might be applied to social work practice, using case examples to help. The three models discussed are the SWOT approach (Strengths, Weaknesses, Opportunities and Threats), a basic systems approach and a more complex ecological-transactional model. We will aim to show these three models can be applied dynamically throughout your work to help you understand and make sense of complex situations and make the task of assessment and decision-making more efficient and more robust.

Chapter 5 looks at three specific tools for developing an analytical mindset. These tools are distinguished from the models in Chapter 4 in that they can be applied in isolation; in other words, they do not form a coherent, overall model of analysis but can be used and adapted in many different ways. We argue that these tools can be used to help practise your analytical skills and in a sense, we might view them as similar to stabilizer wheels on a bike – once you become proficient at thinking more analytically, you may find that the tools have less value for you. The tools we have selected are cultural reviews, needs analysis and decision-trees.

Chapter 6 provides two extended case examples for you to work through and practise on, either on your own or in small groups. These case examples can also be adapted for larger training sessions. We take you through the examples step by step, showing how you can apply the tools and models of the preceding chapters.

Chapter 7 considers the importance of supervision, building on one of our main themes – that good analysis does not happen when social workers try and do it on their own or view analysis as something separate from the rest of their practice. This chapter discusses what we know about how supervision operates in practice and the links between effective supervision and analytical practice.

In **Chapter 8**, the Conclusion, we summarize the book, highlighting what we see as the key lessons and themes. We also look at ways in which practitioners may wish to further develop their skills in specific areas.

We hope you enjoy reading and using the book as much as we have enjoyed writing it.

Key points from this chapter include:

1   Thinking analytically is one of the hardest tasks that social workers are asked to do.
2   Mental effort is similar to physical effort – it saps your energy and it can be tempting to undertake easier tasks (such as gathering information) rather than harder ones (such as thinking analytically).
3   People like to form narratives (or tell stories) to explain what has happened to them and to others – some narratives are easier to challenge and to change than others.
4   Making changes, both in terms of your own practice and in terms of trying to help service users to change, can be very difficult. However, if one is motivated to change, then seemingly difficult changes can occur with surprising ease and speed.

Recommended reading

Heath, C. and Heath, D. (2011) *Switch: How to Change Things When Change is Hard*. London: Random House Business.

Kahneman, D. (2011) *Thinking Fast and Slow*. London: Allen Lane.

Wilson, T. (2011) *Redirect: The Surprising New Science of Psychological Change*. London: Allen Lane.

1 Critical analysis: what, how and why?

Chapter overview

By the end of this chapter, you should understand:

1 What we mean by critical analysis
2 The differences between analysis, summarizing and decision-making
3 The differences between formal and intuitive reasoning
4 What impacts on your ability to undertake critical analysis
5 What good analysis allows us to do

Introduction: what do we mean by critical analysis and an analytical mindset?

In the Introduction, we gave a basic definition of critical analysis. We said that critical analysis means taking a questioning and enquiring view of the information to hand and obtaining a good understanding of a given situation. We would add to this that critical analysis can allow you to understand more clearly what outcomes are available and how best you might achieve them. In this chapter, we will look at critical analysis in more detail and introduce our idea of an analytical mindset, a central idea of the book.

By an analytical mindset, we mean an approach to practice that is repeatedly questioning the information you have, asking what information might be missing and why it might be important, actively hypothesizing and considering different interpretations of the same information (without speculating too widely or wildly). In other words, an analytical mindset is about taking an overall approach to practice and as such, it affects how one writes assessments, interacts with service users and colleagues but especially how one thinks. It is our strongly held view that practitioners need to develop such a mindset in their practice in order to become the best they can at critical analysis and we would compare this approach to one based on the rote learning of certain tasks or pre-determined steps in someone else's analytical method. This is why we have set out our book as more than just a set of tasks for you to follow, although having said this, we do think that there is value in using particular analytical tasks as a way of practising and developing an analytical mindset.

It might help if we described what a practitioner with an analytical mindset would 'look like'. Such a practitioner would recognize that critical analysis is not a discreet step within a wider process – for example, analysis is not 'a stage' of an assessment that follows information gathering. A practitioner with an analytical mindset would approach all elements of their work with a critical and analytical mind. Using the example of a formal assessment process, an analytically minded practitioner would seek to analyse what information is known about the service user before the assessment starts, what information is assumed, what questions the assessment needs to answer and what information is likely to be more or less relevant in answering them. By doing so, a practitioner with an analytical mindset would not only be able to obtain a better understanding of a service user but would also be more efficient. Many social workers and other professionals would readily admit to being very busy and to feeling overworked and would say that they do not have enough time to really reflect on and analyse their practice. Our argument would be that being analytical is a time saver, not a time consumer. By allowing you to focus on the most relevant information from the outset, you can end up saving time by not collecting information in an extemporary way.

We would want to stress that critical analysis is not something that only happens during a formal assessment process. Being able to actively analyse situations as they are happening – for example, during a home visit with a service user – is also something that an analytically minded practitioner would be comfortable with. This would include reflecting on and analysing what you are and are not being told, your emotional reactions to the service user, their emotional reaction to you and the likely narrative being constructed around the home visit (see Nicolas 2012).

Finally, an analytical mindset enables more defensible decision-making. Being 'defensive' in practice is widely acknowledged as being a 'bad thing' but defensiveness is not the same as being defensible. In many practice situations, the degrees of complexity involved are such that there is almost never a clear 'right' answer about what to do. Therefore, in forums such as Courts, tribunals and judicial and Serious Case Reviews, the examination of practice will tend to focus more on the process by which a decision has been made, rather than on the decision itself (although of course, the actual decision taken is far from unimportant). By approaching practice with a distinctly analytical mindset, practitioners will be in a better position to explain how they came to their decisions and thus avoid giving an appearance of having made arbitrary or prejudicial decisions.

In order to develop an analytical mindset, we think that practitioners need to practise the relevant skills (see Chapter 2). If we were to compare the skill of critical analysis with learning a foreign language or a martial art, we would hope to make clear that one cannot learn these types of skills simply from reading books. Book-learning may well form part of the process but it is in the 'doing' that one learns the most, not just from successes but also from mistakes. It is also clear that when learning these types of skills, one needs to start with basic steps before progressing to intermediate and then expert-level proficiency. This is a model that we seek to follow in the book, by introducing ideas and tasks at a basic level, enabling the reader to practise and then progressing towards more complex ideas and tasks.

In summary, we want practitioners to develop analytical mindsets by practising the skills needed for good, critical analysis and we aim to help you do this. A practitioner with an analytical mindset will be more likely to make decisions based on a thorough understanding of a service user, they will instinctively think about the connections and dynamics between different elements, both real and informational, and analytically minded practitioners will have little difficulty in explaining how they have come to their conclusions and decisions.

How does critical analysis differ from summarizing and decision-making?

Analysing something is different from concisely summarizing or making decisions. We will briefly consider why this is the case. A summary tends to involve questions such as 'What is happening?' and 'Who is involved?'. Decisions tend to involve questions such as 'What should we do?'. Critical analysis, on the other hand, is more about addressing questions such as 'Why is this happening?' and 'How is it important?'.

Practice example (summarizing): Daisy

A manager in a child protection team is reading an assessment of a young child, Daisy, who has been referred to the team because of concerns about her presentation and behaviour at school. The social worker concludes their assessment as follows:

> *Daisy is a 4-year-old girl, living with her mother and her mother's boyfriend. Daisy attends a local nursery and they have said that she often appears grubby and her behaviour is withdrawn and she does not speak very much. Daisy's mother is a recovering alcoholic and her mother's boyfriend has a criminal record for vandalism. Daisy and family live in a one bedroom flat and Daisy has to sleep on the sofa in the front room. The flat is quite dirty and there are not many toys for her to play with. Daisy does not have any other family in the local area. Her mother's boyfriend does not work but does not seem to help much with Daisy either. Daisy's mother is clearly not coping very well.*

This may (or may not) be a helpful and concise summary of Daisy's situation but it offers no sense of *why* things are happening. In other words, it does not contain any critical analysis. Think back to the definition above – analysis has to involve an understanding of why something is as it is (or appears to be). The summary of Daisy does not do this. In one sense, it takes us not very much further than what we might expect to know from a referral – the conclusion that Daisy's mother is not coping very well could have been inferred from Daisy's presentation at nursery, something we knew from the referral. The problem is that we are no closer to knowing *why* Daisy's mother (and her boyfriend) are not coping, *why* Daisy is coming to nursery looking 'grubby' and *why* her behaviour is withdrawn. We do have *some* new information, such as that regarding the state of the home, the sleeping arrangements and some information about Daisy's mother (she is a 'recovering' alcoholic) and her mother's boyfriend (he is not working, has a criminal record and is not that involved in caring for Daisy). However, we are not given any sense of *how* and *why* these things might be impacting on Daisy's presentation and behaviour.

As with summarizing, decision-making is related to but distinct from critical analysis. Decision-making rather obviously describes the act of choosing a particular action or course of action. You might argue that critical analysis is also about deciding on a course of action to take but we would argue that the primary difference is that critical analysis does not (or should not) stop once a decision has been made. An analytically minded practitioner will continue to analyse the impact (or lack of impact) of any decisions taken. It has long been established that many people stop considering other options once they have made a clear decision (see Simon 1957) and in many situations, this makes sense. For instance, imagine you are moving home. Once you have decided on a property to buy or rent and have moved in, it would be somewhat odd, perverse even, to continue looking at other properties to see what else you might have bought or rented (we know that many people enjoy browsing estate agents but we are talking here about continuing an active search, viewing properties and so on).

However, in social work and related professions, it can be quite risky to stop considering the options just because a particular decision has been made or course of action taken. To do so can lead to new information being overlooked, especially if that information challenges the original decision and this can lead to practitioners failing to adequately reflect on and critically analyse the impact of their decisions. We know from research that people in highly pressured situations have a tendency to make quick and clear decisions and what often happens is that retrospective justification is then given to the decision (Klein 1999). This approach is risky for social workers and other professionals and in our field of work, quick and clear decisions only have merit if they are good decisions (in contrast to extreme situations, such as battlefields, in which making any decision, as long as it is clear, can be better than waiting). In social work, making the wrong decision can be more harmful in the long run than waiting, critically analysing and then making a better, more informed decision.

Practice example (decision-making): Daisy

The social worker for Daisy decides that the best course of action is to provide Daisy's mother with help for her alcohol misuse, reasoning that perhaps there are times when she is too inebriated to properly care for Daisy and this explains her grubby appearance and withdrawn behaviour. This has the advantage of being a clear plan of action. However, without a critical and effective analysis of the situation, this may well be a waste of time and resources. Based on the summary above, we do not know how or even if Daisy's mother's difficulties with alcohol are affecting her ability to care for Daisy. We also do not know how likely Daisy's mother is to respond positively to such an intervention.

How does analysis happen?

Intuitive and formal reasoning

Having discussed our idea of an analytical mindset and compared summarizing and decision-making with critical analysis, we will now consider the two main ways in which people think – intuitively and consciously.

For a time, there has been an interesting debate among psychologists (and others) about whether people are more intuitive or formal (conscious) in their thought processes and what 'type' of thinking was more important. Intuitive thought is a quick process, often involving assumptions and biases, based on experience and how you feel. Intuitive thought is so fast that people may complete a physical action before – or at the same time as – they become consciously aware of the stimulus for it. For example, the sound of angry shouting will tend to cause people to look in the direction of the sound before they become consciously aware of having heard anything. In this sense, intuition is defined as a type of holistic perspective, taking into account 'all types of information that cannot easily be articulated explicitly' (Pretz 2008: 6).

Conscious thought, on the other hand, is a much slower process and involves weighing up evidence, logic and reason. Intuitive thought can often play a role as a cue for conscious thought. The sound of angry shouting will tend to draw the attention of your intuitive system before your conscious system takes over and decides how to react. However, there can also be situations in which your intuitive system is the decision-maker. For example, you hear the sound of angry shouting, which causes you to intuitively turn towards the noise. As you do so, you intuitively observe a group of apparently angry people running towards you. Your intuitive system is likely to prompt a 'fight or flight' response without waiting for your conscious system to process what has happened.

However, we can also see lots of examples of when the two systems work closely together, even when faced with abstract problems. For example, what is 243×12? There are very few people who can give an exact, intuitive answer to this (although there are some people, often with conditions such as autism and synaesthesia, who report being able to answer these types of questions without conscious thought; see Tammet 2007). Nevertheless, even though it is unlikely you will be able to intuit an exact answer, you may well understand intuitively that the answer will be *in the range of* 2500–3500 and not in the range of, say, 100–500 or 10,000–20,000. Were you presented with multiple choice answers of 541, 2916 or 15,067, you are quite likely to get it right, even if you are only given a few seconds to decide.

However, the two systems do not always work so harmoniously; faced with other problems, they can give quite conflicting 'views' (see Sloman 1996). An example of this can be seen by asking whether the Catholic Pope is a bachelor. Your intuitive response is most likely 'no' because the Pope does not fit with most people's common sense view of a bachelor. And yet, a conscious response is more likely to be 'yes' because the Pope is an unmarried, adult male and therefore, he fits the dictionary definition of a bachelor (Norenzayan et al. 2002).

The key to understanding these two different types of thinking is not to identify which one is 'best' – rather, as we saw in the Introduction, it is to recognize that everyone uses both approaches in almost every area of their lives and each system has *context-dependent* strengths and weaknesses. In other words, depending on the 'problem' being addressed, each system is more or less useful. Sloman (1996) identifies various situations in which each approach can be more useful. For the intuitive (or 'associative') system, Sloman identifies situations of intuition, fantasy, creativity, imagination, visual recognition and associative memory. For example, when a filmmaker edits their new action film, trying to ensure that the pace is exciting, one might expect them to rely primarily on an intuitive approach. For the conscious (or 'rule-based') system, Sloman identifies situations of deliberation, explanation, formal analysis, verification, ascription of purpose and strategic memory. You might expect to see this approach used in a Court of law, perhaps by jurors when they are determining a suspect's guilt or innocence.

Indeed, examining the example of jurors in more detail can tell us a lot about how people actually analyse complex situations and make decisions. Understanding this process, perhaps unsurprisingly, has attracted a great deal of interest from criminal lawyers. By learning how jurors make their decisions, lawyers are able to change how they approach trials and defend their clients (Solomon 2002). What is clear is that jurors are not 'robotic' decision-making machines in the courtroom, anymore than social workers are in their practice.

As we saw in the Introduction, narratives are very important to people and jurors are typically keen to impose a story – an organized narrative – onto the information they are given in a trial (Pennington and Hastie 1991). In practice, this means that if a narrative is not provided for them (for example, by the lawyers), then they will more than likely formulate their own; a story that fits the facts of a case but also fits their own values and beliefs. Facts that 'fit in' with a juror's own values and beliefs are more readily accepted than facts that challenge them. Research has found that jurors, like everyone else, have a hierarchy of values or beliefs, with some 'core' values or beliefs that are not open to change regardless of circumstances and others that are of less importance and are amenable to change, depending on the circumstances. As an example, a fairly common belief for many people is that individuals, once they reach adulthood if not before, are responsible for their own actions. In a criminal trial for assault, the accused may plead guilty but offer a mitigating plea that the victim of the assault was at the time having an extra-marital relationship with his wife. A juror who would not be swayed by this information could be said to hold their belief in personal responsibility as a core value. A juror who felt the information about the extra-marital relationship was a reasonable mitigating circumstance may continue to hold their belief in personal responsibility but for them, it could not be one of their core values, as showed by the reduction in their strength of feeling based on the new circumstantial information (see Covey 2005).

Aside from any facts of the case, jurors have also been found to place a great deal of importance on the (perceived) 'issues' in the case. For example, in a trial about a breach of contract, jurors will take account not only of whether a breach has technically occurred but whether the lawyer who wrote the contact was competent, whether the contract itself was fair and so on. Solomon (2002) draws a comparison with a teenager who is upset because they have a midnight curfew. In the spirit of compromise, the teenager's parents may agree to a curfew of 1 a.m. instead and be surprised when this makes the teenager even more upset. Such a scenario would suggest that the teenager is not, in fact, upset at the particular time of the curfew but at the perceived lack of trust by their parents. In other words, it is the wider issue of even having a curfew that is upsetting the teenager, not the actual time of the curfew per se.

Finally, research with jurors has found that the *order* in which information is presented can have a significant impact on how they understand the case (Wenner and Cusimano 2000). This finding is based on the well-known psychological process in which people generally make sense of new information based on information they already have. In other words, 'first impressions' really do count. This process is similar to that of confirmation bias, a process in which people tend to seek out information that confirms their pre-existing views and to ignore or 'explain away' information that contradicts them (see Munro 1999, 2008).

This research into how jurors analyse court cases and make their decisions gives us several insights into critical analysis for social workers. We have seen how the issue of applying narratives to complex situations can have real effects and how a person's values and beliefs can have at least as strong a bearing on how they understand something as can the cold, hard facts. These two insights suggest that a purely rational, conscious approach to critical analysis is likely to be difficult, if not impossible, to achieve. In the context of social work, this tells us that we need to do more than simply obtain 'facts' about service users – we need to go further and examine values and beliefs and how these colour and shape our views, both for service users but also for ourselves. We have also seen how confirmation bias and the process by which people assess and process new information based on existing information affects the outcome of trials. social work, the risk is that an initial view of a service user can be hard to change.

Overall, by examining some ideas related to conscious and intuitive thinking have seen how both processes are important in how people analyse situations they and problems they encounter. We have also seen that in social work practice, as in areas, we cannot simply 'decide' to be conscious and not intuitive – both systems and integrate with each other. Because of this, it will be useful to understand w you, the reader, are more comfortable with or more likely to use conscious or ir thinking. There is research to suggest that people are at their most creative wh deliberately use the style of thought with which they are *less* comfortable (D. 2011). This has implications for how we approach our practice and how w nudged to come up with novel and potentially more helpful analyses and in helping u to avoid making assumptions about what we mistakenly believe are situations we have encountered before (a kind of meta-confirmation bias).

Research summary: intuitive and conscious thinking

In indirect tests comparing people's intuitive reasoning with analytical tools – such as formal models or equations – intuitive reasoning cannot help but fall short. This is because the analytical tool is used as the standard to be achieved (Hammond et al. 1997). However, this does not mean that in practice, conscious reasoning is always the best approach. A more realistic comparison would be between *one person's* intuitive and *their own* analysis (*relative efficacy*).

The key point is to understand when an intuitive or conscious approach is being used and how best to combine them. Experts often claim to have an intuitive understanding of a complex topic – they 'know' the answer more quickly than could be achieved by more conscious reasoning. However, studies have shown that in terms of judgments made by *professionals not directly affected by the outcome* (such as social workers), these are often seen as requiring more conscious reasoning, not intuition (Sjöberg 2003).

Studies have found that in many situations, combining intuitive and conscious reasoning results in better outcomes (e.g. Selart et al. 2008). It has also been found that in many cases, decision-making does not neatly fall into either intuition or conscious reasoning – most decisions are made following a combination of the two approaches (Croskerry 2009).

'Forcing' oneself to think in an 'unusual' way (i.e. more intuitive thinkers using conscious reasoning and more conscious thinkers using intuition) can lead to an increase in creative thinking and creative approaches to problems (Dane et al. 2011).

Before we move on to the next section, a quick test for you (Exercise 1). If you are unsure whether you are more of a conscious or intuitive thinker, the following cognitive reflection test (CRT) can be a useful way of finding out (the CRT was originally designed by Frederick 2005).

Exercise 1   Cognitive reflection test: are you more inclined towards intuitive or conscious thought?

1   If it takes 5 machines 5 minutes to make 5 widgets, how long would it take 100 machines to make 100 widgets?

   Answer: _____ minutes

2   In a lake, there is a patch of lily pads. Everyday, the patch doubles in size. If it takes 48 days for the patch to cover the entire lake, how long would it take for the patch to cover half the lake?

   Answer: _____ days

3   A bat and ball together cost £1.10. The bat costs £1.00 more than the ball. How much does the ball cost?

   Answer: _____ pence

The CRT is designed so that intuitive answers tend to come to mind more easily than rational answers. Intuitive thinkers are more likely to accept the intuitive answer and move on to the next question; conscious thinkers will tend to take more time over each question before moving on. If you gave the rational answers for two out of the three questions or more, then you are most likely a conscious thinker by preference; if you gave only one or no rational answers, then you are most likely an intuitive thinker by preference. The answers can be found in Appendix 1.

Our understanding of an analytical mindset is that the best type of critical analysis incorporates both conscious, rational thinking and more emotionally guided or intuitive thinking – our argument is that a purely rational approach or a purely intuitive approach is not sufficient to the task of undertaking critical analysis in complex fields such as social work (see Munro 2009).

What affects the quality of analysis?

In this section, we will briefly consider some of the factors that impact on the quality of critical analysis and some of the barriers to being analytically minded in practice.

Practical factors

One of the main issues that practitioners cite when asked why they struggle with critical analysis is a lack of time and it is undoubtedly true that social workers and other professionals are often – if not always – under a great deal of time pressure. Social workers and others have frequently complained to us that they do not have enough time to really get into the kind of analysis and reflection they know is needed. This tends to lead to the overuse of intuitive judgement, as it is a quicker way of thinking than a more conscious approach (see the CRT test above and Helm 2011). This particular issue – of time constraint – is one of the primary reasons why we want to stress the idea of an analytical mindset, rather than seeing critical analysis as (yet) another task for practitioners to cram into an already busy working day. If analysis is approached as a stand-alone task, something to be completed on your own, probably in front of a computer, then it will take a long time and it will be incredibly difficult. As we saw in the Introduction, mental effort is like physical effort and consumes real energy from the body. Working alone in a very time-pressured job on such a demanding task is, in essence, impossible. So if you have tried to do your critical analysis in this way and have found it difficult, do not worry too much! We aim to show, instead, how critical analysis can save you time and how it is best thought of as a state of mind, something to be undertaken in conjunction with other people, whether with colleagues, services users or both.

Another issue often raised is that of the complexity of social work. This is often highlighted in official reports and inquiries and the sheer complexity of practice can be overwhelming and really challenge the possibility of ever being amenable to good, critical analysis. We would seek only to note that the more complex the work, the better one needs to be at critical analysis and indeed, not only can critical analysis save time but it can help reduce feelings of being overwhelmed by making the complexity easier to understand.

Other practical factors often cited as an impediment to critical analysis are a lack of knowledge of theory or research and a focus in social work training and education on client-centred approaches without the necessary attention to communication skills (Helm 2011). We will consider the skills needed for critical analysis in the next chapter and this will include a consideration of communication skills and the need to be research minded.

Personal factors

It is unavoidable that our own life experiences will impact on how we think, reason and analyse situations at work. As we saw in the Introduction and in the discussion of jurors in this chapter, our own values and beliefs are so influential as to affect how we interpret apparently objective facts. Two individuals with two different sets of values and beliefs could end up with very different views of the same situation. This is a long-term factor, influenced by early relational experiences, the culture we grew up in and live in and by our experiences of adult relationships, among many other factors. However, there are also short-term personal factors that will have an impact on the quality of our analytical thinking. Everyone's moods tend to change and fluctuate over a given period of time, whether that is a day, a week or a month. Something as relatively simple and common as being stuck in traffic and running late for an appointment will influence how you feel when you arrive. You may feel more rushed and less inclined towards patience and empathy. Such things are unavoidable in the real world but cannot be discounted in terms of how we interpret and analyse information.

Organizational factors

Finally, organizational factors such as the openness or defensiveness of our agencies and the level of 'group-think' we experience can also influence how we analyse. The role of supervision in this process is key. As we have already suggested, it is best to think about critical analysis as something you do in combination with other people, rather than something you do on your own, in front of a computer in a busy office. In other words, good critical analysis is most likely to happen via communication and in conjunction with other people, through discussion of your intuitions and rational views, of the information have and do not have and the different hypotheses that could explain what is going on.

What does critical analysis help us to do?

The expectation that social workers in all fields will undertake critical analysis and the crucial role of analysis in good practice is made clear by various pieces of government guidance. However, as already noted, guidance such as *The Framework for the Assessment of Children in Need and Their Families*, tends to contribute to the misguided view that analysis is something that happens *after* you have collected the information. The Framework says 'gathering information is a crucial phase in the assessment process' (paragraph 4.6, p. 54) followed by 'summarising' and 'then analysis' (paragraphs 4.7 and 4.9, pp. 54 and 55). However, we wish to challenge this view and argue instead that an analytically minded practitioner would make no such distinction. This is in large part because it is not possible to collect information in a neutral way and then analyse it at some later point. As we saw with jurors, the order in which information is presented (or collected) is significant but you also have to decide which information to collect and which information to leave out. Therefore, some level of analysis has already happened before you even begin and it is much better for this analysis to be done explicitly rather than implicitly. We would expect an analytically minded practitioner to be aware of the choices they make when deciding which information to collect.

Therefore, in response to the challenge that a lack of time precludes good, critical analysis, we say that good, critical analysis saves time. How? By helping you be more efficient in terms of the information you gather. Starting from the premise that no practitioner can claim to collect *all* the available information, there must always be a degree of selection that takes place. By thinking analytically from the outset, you will be in a better position to 'know' which information to collect, which information is likely to be more or less significant and to be clearer about what questions you are seeking to answer. Think of it this way – if someone was assessing your family and they asked you to tell them about your childhood, what would you tell them? To literally tell them everything about your childhood would take an inordinately long time, even if it were actually possible to do so (which it would not be). Even if you could tell someone literally everything that happened in your childhood, this would not necessarily lead to a good assessment of how you *experienced* your childhood and how it affects you in the present. More than likely, if asked this question, you would pick out key events that you felt were of particular significance (perhaps you moved home as a teenager and had to separate from your first serious boyfriend or girlfriend) or you might pick out an event which you felt gave a good 'flavour' of your childhood (perhaps describing in detail a family holiday as an example of the 'type' of childhood you think you had).

One might object at this stage that without knowing in advance all of the information about a service user, how could you know what information was significant or not? In reality, no practitioner will ever know all the information about a service user so in this sense, we are not asking practitioners to choose between finding out all the information or being selective – social work is always selective and therefore, we are saying that rather than being selective implicitly and without a clear purpose, one should aim to be selective in an explicit and purposeful way. In addition to this, analytically minded practitioners will be drawing on research knowledge, which can guide us in understanding the type of information likely to be more significant for individual service users. For example, attachment theory teaches us that early relational history is significant in terms of later relationships, or rather a person's current narrative or understanding of their early relational history is significant. By using research and thinking analytically, we can learn to focus our information gathering as efficiently as possible and thus, save time.

Another way of viewing the benefits of critical analysis is in the way it helps us be open and transparent about our decision-making. As we have noted, such is the complexity of much of social work practice that it is difficult to ever claim that a certain decision is exclusively right and all other decisions wrong. Rather, it is almost always about making the best available decision at the time. Therefore, an important aspect of practice is being able to explain and 'defend' the decisions made, as opposed to simply justifying them as being 'right'. We are thinking here of being able to be open and transparent with service users directly but also being able to 'defend' decisions in forums such as court or tribunals. Many decisions may be defensible on the basis that they were reached in a reasonable way even if a court or other official body is minded to overturn the decision. For example, in hearings related to the deprivation of a person's liberty (Mental Capacity Act 2005, Mental Health Act 2007), a tribunal may consider whether decisions were made in an arbitrary way and if so, they will likely find such a decision was unlawful. However, if one can demonstrate that the decision was based on a reasonable consideration of the available information, then although the decision may still be overturned, there is unlikely to be any criticism made of the prac-titioner. This is not to say that decisions themselves are irrelevant – clearly, they are highly relevant – but to recognize that the process of how decisions are made is relevant as well.

This leads us to the final positive of using good, critical analysis – it enables us, in consultation with service users, to identify more clearly what we need or are trying to achieve and how best to get there. Thinking back to the example of Daisy (see pp. 13–14), if our overall aim is to improve the care she receives, then we need to start from an understanding of why the current care is sub-standard (or is it?). Describing *what* Daisy's mother is doing – perhaps she is drinking a lot of alcohol – is less useful than under-standing *how* this affects her ability to care for Daisy. If we can be clear exactly how alcohol consumption impacts on Daisy's care, then we can be more confident in taking steps to address it. If, however, we only *assume* that alcohol consumption is the main reason for the sub-standard care, then any attempts to intervene could be a waste of resources and therefore, an inefficient use of time and money.

Exercise 2 What outcomes?

This exercise will help you to think clearly about what outcomes you are trying to achieve. As we saw above, being clear about outcomes is one of the key parts of engaging in good, critical analysis. This could be done individually or in pairs or small groups.

You receive a referral for a 21-year-old woman, Angie. The referral informs you that Angie lives at home with her mother and father and her two sisters. Angie and her sisters are triplets. The referral is received from Angie's mother and is asking for your help to re-house Angie out of the area because Angie's mother is concerned that her behaviour is becoming more difficult and dangerous to manage. You meet with Angie and her parents and they inform you that Angie often goes out without telling anyone where she is going and does not return until late at night. On several occasions, the family have reported Angie as missing to the police, who later returned her home unharmed. Angie's parents inform you that if they try and stop Angie going out, she becomes aggressive. Angie tells you she used to attend a further education college but she no longer wants to go; she wants to spend time with her friends instead. Angie's parents tell you that her 'friends' are actually using her to help deal cannabis for them and Angie does not realize she is being taken advantage of. Angie refuses to talk any more about her friends, saying that no one understands.

Now answer the following questions:

1   What outcomes do you think Angie's parents might want from the referral?
2   What outcomes do you think Angie might want from the referral, if any?
3   What outcomes would you, as a social worker, want from the referral?
4   In what ways do the outcomes you have identified contradict each other? How would you decide which outcomes to prioritize?

You can see an example of how we completed this exercise in Appendix 2 (see also Wilkins 2012).

Summary and conclusions

What does any of this mean for social work practice? There are several conclusions that we would like to draw. In the Introduction, we saw how mental activity takes real effort and we have also noted how difficult critical analysis usually is, especially when dealing with some of the complex problems that practitioners routinely encounter. Therefore, it is not surprising that many people find analytical thinking to be so difficult – after all, it would not surprise us if many practitioners had difficulty in running a 10km race either (especially if they did not prepare well enough!).

We have also looked at the two main systems of thinking, intuitive and conscious, and noted how we cannot simply 'decide' to use one or the other but that we must learn how to use them both. We have seen the importance of being able to discuss intuitive reactions with colleagues and service users, so as to ensure that the quick and simple views or narratives that often come to mind are not simply accepted unchallenged. We have also looked at how our values and beliefs and our innate need to construct simple narratives can affect how we think about and analyse situations. We have noted the importance of being aware of values, beliefs and narratives and how this has the potential to help us think more clearly and to note where these factors are impacting on our analytical thinking. We have also seen how our ability to engage in good, critical analysis is not just within our own control – it is affected by factors such as time pressure, team environment and the abilities of our colleagues to do the same.

Finally, we have seen how good, critical analysis has the potential to help save us time, to be more open with service users, to understand the 'hows' and 'whys' of situations, to think more clearly about the outcomes available and to choose the most likely course(s) of action to achieve those outcomes. We have also seen how critical analysis needs to take account not only of information that is known, but information that may be unknown. The 'Rumsfeldian' idea of 'known knowns' (things we know we know), 'known unknowns' (things we know we do not know) and 'unknown unknowns' (things we do not know we do not know) is surprisingly apt.

Exercise 3   Known unknowns

This exercise will help you think about the importance of what information is left out, why this might be and how this can change and colour your understanding of an event or situation.

1   Select a well-known story from the national news – it does not matter which type of story you select. You could choose something related to a political scandal, a piece of economic news, a sports story or a story about a celebrity. You then need to select two different news organizations (such as the *Daily Telegraph* and the *Guardian* or the BBC news website and ITV news website) which have both reported on the same story.

2   Read both reports of the same story from the two different organizations and compare what you learn about the story from each one. You might find it helpful to note this down somewhere.

3   Now think about what information has *not* been included in the stories. You might be able to identity information that is included in one report but not the other. You might be able to infer what information or what type of information has been left out of both stories by applying your general knowledge of these types of stories to these individual examples.

4   Once you have completed your two lists – the information included and what information has not been included – see if you can explain why this might be the case. Why is certain information felt to be important enough to be included and why might other pieces of information be considered superfluous? Feel free to speculate, as you may not be able to answer for certain.

5   Finally, think about whether the information that has been left out could have changed your view of the story if it had been included. If so, how and why? As with question 4, some speculation may be required.

You can see an example of how we completed this exercise in Appendix 3.

Key points from this chapter include:

- Summarizing information is a key part of analysis but analysis is more than providing a good summary.
- Critical analysis is not a separate part of practice – an analytical mindset needs to underpin everything we do.
- Without good analysis, it is unlikely you will be able to make sound judgements and make the best available decisions.
- Being aware of values and beliefs and the narratives we and others construct is an important part of critical analysis.

Recommended reading

Munro, E. (1999) Common errors of reasoning in child protection work, *Child Abuse and Neglect*, 23: 745–58. http://eprints.lse.ac.uk/358/) (accessed June 2012).

Munro, E. (2009) Guide to analytic and intuitive reasoning, *Community Care Inform*. http://www.ccinform.co.uk/Articles/2009/08/20/3390/Guide+to+analytic+and+intuitive+reasoning.html (accessed June 2012).

Nicolas, J. (2012) *Conducting the Home Visit in Child Protection*. Maidenhead: Open University Press.

2 Skills for critical analysis

Chapter overview

By the end of this chapter, you should have an understanding of:

- The skills needed for critical analysis
- What each of these skills entails
- Your own strengths and areas of development
- How you can work on developing each of these skills

Introduction

The usual procedure for official reports concerning social work practice (such as Laming's inquiries following the deaths of Victoria Climbié and Peter Connolly in 2003 and 2009; Laming 2003, 2009) is to identify the flaws in practice and make various recommendations to address them. What is often missing is a consideration of the skills that social workers and others might need in order to achieve the recommendations (Keys 2009a, 2009b). For example, in his first report, Laming recommended that professionals need to make clear referrals when they are worried about children. This is a good recommendation! After all, no one would advocate making 'unclear' referrals but the report does not give any indication of what skills might be needed in order to make a clear referral. Therefore, we have included a chapter on the skills that we think underpin critical analysis in order to avoid making the same mistake. We have tried to set out, using practical advice, how you might practise these skills and how they will contribute to your overall analytical mindset. Remember, as with learning a foreign language or martial art, you will need to do more than just read about these skills – the key is to practise!

Key skills for critical analysis

In 2009, Keys looked at the issue of social work skills and was surprised to find only six studies in all the relevant literature with the express aim of identifying or evaluating key skills for social workers. Keys did find a further 127 articles that gave at least some consideration to skills but only the original six considered the relationship between skills and practice. Although this literature search took place a few years ago now, it does appear to us that there remains a significant gap in our knowledge and understanding of how skills relate to good practice outcomes.

Fortunately, there is rather more research regarding the skills of critical analysis (although not necessarily in the field of social work). For example, Platt (2011) identified the skills of hypothesizing and clear writing and in addition to this, we have identified the skills of time management, critical understanding, research-mindedness, communication (which includes clear writing skills) and reflection and we will now consider each of these skills in turn.

Time management

We have discussed the issue of time in the previous chapter and we said that, anecdotally, we often hear from practitioners about the time pressure they feel under. This appears to be a common theme. For example, the final report of the Social Work Task Force (Social Work Reform Board 2009) noted that social workers repeatedly said that they do not have enough time to work directly with the people they want to help. The same report says that newly qualified social workers are often inadequately prepared for the demands of their role. We also know from earlier research that social workers, teachers and nurses have all said that trying to manage their time effectively is one of the most stressful parts of their job (Klas and Hawkins 1997). We also know that increased levels of stress negatively affect how clearly people can think (e.g. Janis and Mann 1976; McEwan and Sapolsky 1995; Stewart et al. 1999 and Braunstein-Bercovitz et al. 2001).

Given this, focusing on improving skills of time management potentially allows for a virtuous circle of more efficient working, leading to lower stress levels, leading to better critical analysis (clearer thinking). As we have already argued, better critical analysis will in turn allow you to use your time more efficiently and thus complete the virtuous circle.

Exercise 4 How good is your time management?

Questions	Not at all	Rarely	Sometimes	Often	Very often
1 Are the tasks you work on during the day the ones with the highest priority?					
2 Do you find yourself completing tasks at the last minute, or asking for extensions?					
3 Do you set aside time for planning and scheduling?					
4 Do you know how much time you are spending on the various jobs you do?					
5 How often do you find yourself dealing with interruptions?					
6 Do you use goal setting to decide what tasks and activities you should work on?					
7 Do you leave contingency time in your schedule to deal with 'the unexpected'?					
8 Do you know whether the tasks you are working on are high, medium or low value?					
9 When you are given a new assignment, do you analyse it for importance and prioritize it accordingly?					
10 Are you stressed about deadlines and commitments?					
11 Do distractions often keep you from working on critical tasks?					
12 Do you find you have to take work home, in order to get it done?					
13 Do you prioritize your 'To Do' list or Action Programme?					
14 Do you regularly confirm your priorities with your boss?					
15 Before you take on a task, do you check that the results will be worth the time put in?					

Scoring

Each answer is worth 1, 2, 3, 4 or 5 points. For questions 1, 3, 4, 6, 7, 8, 9, 13, 14 and 15, the scoring runs left to right (Not at all = 1 point, Very often = 5 points) and for questions 2, 5, 10, 11 and 12 the scoring runs right to left (Not at all = 5 points, Very often = 1 point).

Score interpretation

Score	Comments
46–75	You have very good time management skills!
31–45	You are good in some areas but there is room for improvement in others.
15–30	Oh dear! In a positive light, you have a lot of potential for improving your time management skills.

What to do now?

Questions 6, 10, 14 and 15 relate to goal setting, questions 1, 4, 8, 9, 13, 14 and 15 to prioritization (operating a 'to do' list based on importance rather than ease of the task), questions 5, 9, 11 and 12 to managing interruptions, questions 2, 10 and 12 to procrastination ('I'll do that later') and questions 3, 7 and 12 to scheduling of time. If you review your answers, you should be able to work out in which areas you scored best and on which areas you might need to focus to improve your overall time management.

N.B. The above quiz is taken from the excellent website www.mindtools.com, where you can find lots more information on time management and related issues such as problem solving, project management and career skills. We highly recommend it.

Having had a chance to review your current time management skills, what can be done to help improve them? We are going to look at two simple ideas.

'To do' lists

'To do' lists are a very common way of organizing one's time. The problem is that they tend to be very general and they tend to be hard to manage effectively. A typical practitioner's 'to do' list might look something like this:

1 Telephone Dr Smith
2 Arrange visit to see Harry
3 Book supervision
4 Write to Linda
5 Confirm time and location for multi-agency meeting BY FRIDAY

The problem with this kind of 'to do' list is that it lacks any context (why do I need to visit Harry?) and there is no clear sense of priority (should I call Dr Smith first or write to Linda?). It is also, obviously, just a list of tasks and the danger for practitioners in highly complex fields such as social work is that it can become tempting to measure the quality of work by the number of tasks completed, rather than being outcome focused. There is also a risk that the focus will be more on achievable tasks, easier tasks if you will, than more complex or potentially tricky ones. If the visit to Harry is likely to involve a highly emotionally charged situation, it could be, understandably to some degree, tempting to do all of the other tasks first.

A simple but effective improvement to 'to do' lists is to start with projects and attach tasks to them, rather than just listing tasks. The aim of this is for each project to represent an outcome you are seeking and the tasks to be the things you need to do in order to achieve the outcome. By keeping the outcome at the forefront of your 'to do' list, it also becomes easier to evaluate your performance against things that really matter. You also need to ensure that the content of each task is slightly more developed, so it is clear how each one relates to the overall project (or outcome). So, how might this look in practice? For a child protection social worker, it might look something like this:

1   Project: Keep Harry safe from domestic violence in his home
    a   Visit Harry at home to ask him how he feels about dad visiting
    b   Write to Linda to ask for an update on Harry's mother's engagement with the domestic violence service
    c   Book supervision to review whether Harry is safe enough at home
    d   Arrange multi-agency meeting – to bring together all the agencies working with Harry and family BY FRIDAY.
    e   Telephone Dr Smith – has he seen Harry's dad recently and is the anger management programme making progress?

Of course, putting together such a list will take slightly more time but we believe it would be time well spent for the reasons we outlined above. We would invite you to try this in your own practice and see what difference it makes for you.

Kanban boards

A Kanban board can be thought of as a more developed 'to do' list. The difference between a regular 'to do' list and a Kanban board is that the latter includes a visual representation of the priority of different tasks. Figure 2.1 gives an example of the previous 'to do' list, reformatted into a Kanban board.

The idea would be that you use something like stick-it notes for the tasks, so they can be moved around or removed as required and so that new tasks can be added. The advantage of this, over a traditional 'to do' list, is that a visual indication of priority can be given to each task. It also includes a section 'for review', which can be a useful way of reminding you to not just 'complete' a task but to review the outcome of it. For example,

URGENT	1	2	3	4
Backlog	To start	In progress	Nearly complete	For review
	Confirm multi-agency meeting	Arrange visit to see Harry		
Telephone Dr Smith		Book supervision		
				Write to Linda

Figure 2.1   A Kanban board (a type of visual 'to do' list)

simply writing to Linda to ask for an update is not in-and-of-itself of any value. Indicating the task is 'for review' can act as a prompt to not only chase up a response (if one is not forthcoming) but to take account of the information that Linda provides. Again, this approach can at least initially take more time than a traditional 'to do' list but we perceive the benefits to be worthwhile. We also know that once you become more experienced at using them, adding and moving tasks around is actually very quick and easy.

Abductive reasoning *or* hypothesizing

Most people are probably aware of the skill of abductive reasoning without realizing it. Sherlock Holmes, the fictional detective, famously uses the skill of abductive reasoning although he refers to it – inaccurately – as deductive reasoning. Using 'deduction' (actually, abduction), Holmes demonstrates his abilities to solve complex crimes that have proved beyond the abilities of more mundane detectives. In the modern BBC series, *Sherlock*, viewers are given a visual representation of Holmes's abilities. When Holmes meets certain characters, the camera assumes his point of view and viewers are thus shown how Holmes notices things that allow him to deduce even more. For example, Holmes may see small white hairs on a character's trousers and deduce that they own a small white-haired dog. Seconds later, Holmes will notice a slightly different looking hair on the same pair of trousers and deduce that the character actually owns two small dogs. This is abductive reasoning, whereby you make reasonable conclusions based on what you know or observe.

    The difference between deductive and abductive reasoning is as follows – deductive reasoning involves the construction of arguments in which conclusions *necessarily* follow, given a premise or set of premises. The following is a famous example of deductive reasoning:

Premise 1:	All men are mortal.
Premise 2:	Socrates is a man.
Conclusion:	Socrates is mortal.

The conclusion that Socrates is mortal must be true if the two premises are true. In other words, there is no way that the conclusion cannot be true, if the two premises are true. Abductive reasoning, on the other hand, involves drawing reasonable hypotheses (probably true) rather than necessary conclusions (must be true). We can set out the Holmes example of the supposed dog owner as follows:

Premise 1:	This person has small white hairs on his trouser legs.
Premise 2:	Dogs leave small white hairs on trouser legs.
Hypothesis:	It is likely that this person owns a dog or dogs.

Hopefully, the difference between this example and the Socrates example is clear – in this second example, the hypothesis is not *necessarily* true (there are other reasons why someone might have small white hairs on their trouser legs) but it is a *reasonable* hypothesis, nevertheless. Let's look at some more examples and develop this idea a bit further.

Premise:	The lawn is wet this morning.
Hypothesis:	It rained recently.

The hypothesis that it rained recently is a reasonable one based on the information we have (the premise). However, it is not the only reasonable hypothesis and furthermore, new information may well change your view on what would and would not be reasonable. For example:

Premise:	The lawn is wet.
Premise:	There is a sprinkler on the lawn.
Hypothesis 1:	The sprinkler has been used recently.
Or	
Hypothesis 2:	It rained recently.

You might then decide to gather further information to help disconfirm one or both of these hypotheses. In this example, you might check whether the shed, the garden swing, the path and the windows of the house are also wet. If they were all wet, as well as the lawn, you might decide that it is more reasonable to conclude it has been raining than that the sprinkler has been on.

Using this kind of example, abductive reasoning or hypothesizing seems quite simple and in many ways, it is. We were able to construct two plausible hypotheses for why the lawn was wet and to think of what new information might help us decide which hypothesis was more reasonable or likely. If there were still a question mark over which one was more likely, then it would not be too difficult to think of what new information one could seek (such as whether the neighbours' lawn was wet or dry).

Munro (2008) argues that we should take a similar approach to social work practice, generating reasonable hypotheses based on the available information and then seeking new information to disconfirm (rule out) each hypothesis. This is an important point – we should not seek information to *confirm* our hypotheses but to disconfirm them. Munro argues that the risk of only seeking information that confirms our preferred hypothesis is that of confirmation bias, the tendency people have to overlook or 'explain away' information that contradicts our own view and to too readily accept information which confirms it.

Similar to Munro, we argue that in order to work more analytically, practitioners need to be comfortable with generating and being explicit about their hypotheses and using these as a basis for asking further questions. Another way of thinking about the same issue is to try and identify what are known as 'counter factuals'. A counter factual is a grammatical form related to logic or philosophy but in essence, counter factuals are statements that would be true if certain premises were also true. An example will hopefully make this a bit clearer:

Premise:	If the grass were not wet
Counter-factual:	then it cannot have been raining.

Here are some more examples:

Premise:	If Neil Armstrong had not been the first person to walk on the moon
Counter-factual:	then someone else would have been.

Premise:	If Daisy's mother's alcohol use is the sole reason for her poor care of Daisy
Counter-factural:	then Daisy should receive better care when her mother drinks less.

The benefit of counter factuals is that they too can help you think about what more information you might need. In the third example of Daisy, the counter factual helps us think about gathering specific information on when Daisy's mother drinks and then comparing this to Daisy's presentation when she goes to school. It is only by being explicit about hypotheses and counter factuals that we can hope to explore them more fully.

Exercise 5   Generating hypotheses

This exercise will help you think about generating more than one hypothesis and understanding what information you might want to find in order to disconfirm them. Please read the following case example:

You are a social worker in a child protection team. You receive a referral and are asked to carry out an initial assessment with a view to deciding whether a formal child protection investigation needs to take place or not.

   Robbie, a 14-year-old boy, is referred by his school as they are concerned that he might be out of parental control. The school reports that Robbie is frequently late to school, that on a few occasions he has arrived appearing to be under the influence of drugs or alcohol and that he has become isolated from his peers. The school says they have tried to visit Robbie's parents at home but have been unable to contact them to arrange such a visit. The school counsellor has spoken with Robbie and he denies using drugs or alcohol but said he is on prescription medication that can cause drowsiness. Robbie says that his parents recently separated and that his younger brother has been diagnosed with autism. Robbie says that he is often late as he has to help get him ready in the mornings since his dad left. However, during a PE lesson, school staff noticed what appeared to be bite marks and cigarette burns on Robbie's back and legs. Robbie said that he caused the cigarette burns as (he said he has recently taken up smoking) and the bite marks are actually caused by Robbie practising martial arts using his nun-chucks.

1   What is your initial, intuitive reaction? Is Robbie being abused/neglected or not (do not 'over think' this question – give the first, honest answer that comes to your mind)?
2   Formulate a hypothesis that describes the information above with the conclusion that Robbie is being abused/neglected (think back to the example of the wet lawn – we concluded that it had rained last night because the sprinkler could not have reached all the way to the windows).

3   Now formulate a hypothesis that explains the information above but with the conclusion that Robbie is not being abused/neglected.

Reflection point

Think back to the skill of time management. We have argued that critical analysis helps you to save time by thinking more clearly about what information you need to collect. Depending on the hypotheses you think plausible, you will want to collect different information to confirm or disconfirm them. By being explicit about your hypotheses before conducting an assessment, you can save yourself time by not seeking out irrelevant information.

4   Finally, for each hypothesis you have, think of one piece of information that, if it were true, would discount it. If you cannot think of one piece of information that would absolutely discount the hypothesis, try and think of one piece of information that would at least strongly challenge the hypothesis.

You can see an example of how we completed this exercise in Appendix 4.

Research-mindedness

The skill of research-mindedness refers to two things: being aware of research but also the ability to be critically reflective about it. Being aware of research is one thing but being able to reflect on the strengths and weaknesses of individual pieces of research and identifying how to make use of relevant findings in practice is the real skill (Orme and Shemmings 2010). Finding pieces of research is relatively easy, especially with the advent of search engines such as *Google Scholar*, but this can create or increase the temptation to justify hypotheses or decisions after the fact. As we saw in the section above, only seeking information to confirm your view can be risky. Let's quickly delve into a practical example.

Practice example: using research and the risk of confirmation bias

You are a mental health social worker and a service user informs you that they have been hearing voices. You sensitively ask them to describe what the voices are telling them and they say that the voices are present quite often, that they do not overly trouble the service user and that they sometimes make sense and sometimes do not. This concerns you and as a social worker with a belief in the value of research, you decide to search Google Scholar for 'why do people hear voices?'. We carried out this search in January 2012 and the top result was a paper by Barrett and Etheridge (1992) entitled 'Verbal hallucinations in normals, I: People who hear voices'. This paper describes a study in which it was found that a significant minority of college students reported verbal hallucinations, with nearly half of these respondents hearing voices at least once a month. These verbal hallucinations were not found to be related to any symptoms of psychopathology and essentially, these respondents were 'normal' individuals. This study reassures you that you do not need to do any further work with the service user, other than reassuring them that what they are experiencing is fairly common and that they should contact you again if they do begin to feel troubled by the voices. You might also put the service user in contact with an organization such as the Hearing Voices Network (http://www.hearing-voices.org/) should you feel this appropriate.

On the face of it, what is wrong with this approach? The problem is that although the social worker has shown an appreciation for the value of research and how to find a potentially relevant paper, he or she has shown no critical reflection of the research and has made no attempt to find any research evidence that would contradict the fairly benign view of the service user hearing voices. One might estimate that the underlying (implicit) hypothesis of the social worker is that the hearing of voices is a factor to be explained, rather than a cause for concern. This may well be accurate (and indeed a wider survey of the research would seem to confirm this). However, what if the social worker had a different underlying hypothesis – that hearing voices is cause for grave concern?

Practice example: using research and the risk of confirmation bias

In this example, the same service user approaches a different social worker and reports the same concern – that they have been hearing voices. This social worker searches Google Scholar for 'hearing voices risk'. We carried out this search in January 2012 and the top result was a paper by Escher et al. (2002) entitled 'Formation of delusional ideation in adolescents hearing voices: a prospective study'. This study followed a group of 80 adolescents who reported hearing voices and found that, after three years, 50 per cent were in receipt of professional mental health care and 16 per cent showed evidence of delusional ideation (a delusion is a false belief and ideation is the creation of new ideas – in other words, the creation of false beliefs). This paper might concern you, perhaps suggesting that there is a 50 per cent chance that the service user will need professional mental health care within three years and a fairly significant chance that delusional ideation could occur. Your course of action now might be to recommend that professional mental health care begin immediately, given the likelihood of it starting anyway, and in order to lower the risk that delusional ideation would follow.

It is not hard to see how these two different responses would feel very different for the service user, potentially impacting on areas such as their view of themselves (am I mentally unwell or not?), their job or job prospects and their family and social relationships. The point we are making is not that either of these two papers is 'right' or 'wrong' but that giving undue weight to either paper in isolation can quite easily feed into and confirm (confirmation bias) a pre-existing viewpoint.

So how might you develop a level of research-mindedness that includes an awareness of research but also a critical and reflective approach? Being aware of research is really down to you – we would recommend that you become familiar with such resources as Google Scholar, Community Care Inform and the Social Care Institute for Excellence (SCIE) to keep abreast of developments in research. The latter two especially are designed for use by social care practitioners and are very accessible. However, you do need to bear in mind the importance of doing more than simply looking for research to confirm your view – it would actually be better to deliberately look for research to disconfirm your view.

The following reflection point offers a checklist for evaluating individual studies or papers.

Reflection point: how to evaluate research studies and papers

1   Is what is being claimed potentially refutable? What would disprove the claim or theory?
2   What is the 'riskiness' of what is being claimed? How specific are the claims? Stronger theories tend to make more specific predictions that can potentially be refuted.
3   What attempts have been made to test a claim or theory? The more tests, the stronger the claim (assuming it has not been disproven).
4   Consider how you would feel if the claim or theory was true. Social workers tend to prefer certain explanations, such as the idea that schizophrenia is the product of social and family factors (Laing 1990), than other types of explanations, such as the idea that schizophrenia is genetically determined (Eysenck 1960). You should be wary of dis-regarding ideas simply because you do not 'like them' or they do not 'fit' with what you see as your professional background.
5   Consider clarity of expression – the more clearly an idea can be expressed, the less ambiguous it often is.

We particularly like the following example (taken from Dawkins 1998) – we find it difficult to think how this could be made clear and we also have no idea what it means! *'We can clearly see that there is no bi-univocal correspondence between linear signifying links or archi-writing, depending on the author, and this multi-referential, multi-dimensional machine catalysis.'*

Exercise 6   How research minded are you?

Questions	Not at all	Partly	Very well
I understand the important and relevance of research to social work practice			
I understand the broad principles involved in research			
I understand the ethical issues involved in research			
I know how to access, understand and summarize research studies			
I know how to identify research which is relevant to practice in which I am involved			
I know how to relate research to practice issues and demonstrate how relevant research informs my practice			

(Reproduced with permission from the Social Care Institute for Excellence. This self-assessment tool is taken from the SCIE website 'Research Mindedness in Social Work and Social Care'. The link to this site can be found under the Recommended reading section of this chapter.)

Communication

The importance of having good communication skills in the field of social worker is widely accepted but perhaps most importantly, the National Occupational Standards for Social Work in the UK includes a statement from service users and carers. From the point of view of people coming into contact with social workers, their priorities are for social workers to clearly explain their role, inform them of what they are doing or plan to do, give clear information, be honest and open about what they can and cannot do, talk to those requiring services directly, take account of issues such as culture and ethnicity and – overall – build honest relationships. None of these things would seem possible without good communication skills.

However, although the importance of good communication is clear, we want to examine particularly the link between good communication skills and good critical analysis. As with the skill of time management, there is a potentially virtuous bi-directional relationship between good communication and critical analysis. Poor analysis seems to lead to a greater difficulty in communicating while good analysis often informs the ability to communicate clearly. Forrester et al. (2008) completed a study looking at how social workers talk to parents about possible child protection concerns and what they found was worrying. Forrester et al. presented social workers with two scenarios and asked them to demonstrate, with an actor playing the part of a parent, how they would talk about the concerns. The social workers in the study tended to ask closed questions, they rarely showed any level of reflection and they also showed low levels of empathy. In response to this, the 'parents' tended to become more resistant and to share less information, especially in response to low levels of empathy. Some readers may wonder whether showing a potentially abusive or neglectful parent high levels of empathy might impair the ability to identify and discuss concerns but this was not the case. Instead, Forrester et al. found that using a highly empathic response together with a clear explanation of the concerns was the best way to encourage the parent to engage and to provide more information.

Exercise 7   Empathic responses

Consider the following scenario (taken from Forrester et al. 2008):

A 5-year-old child is the subject of a child protection plan as a result of his parent being found drunk when he was in her care, poor school attendance and underperformance at school. Despite the child protection plan, the child continues to miss a lot of school and school staff report that the parent often appears to be under the influence of alcohol when she collects him. The parent has also been missing appointments with her alcohol counsellor.

> *An example of a potential conversation between a social worker and the parent could be as follows (this is our example, not one taken from the study). In this example, imagine this is the first time this social worker has met this parent:*

Social worker: *I've come today to talk to you about some reports from the school. They say that yesterday and on several previous occasions actually, you have appeared drunk when collecting your son. Could you tell me about what happened from your point of view?*

Parent: *Yes, well. They would say that. That school have got it in for me. What you lot don't understand is that it's very stressful, being a mum, and actually . . . well if you must know, I'm on medication. Pills from the doctor for my nerves. Sometimes I take them in the day and they make me feel, you know, a bit wobbly and that must be what happened when I went to get him.*

1   What would you say in response to the parent in practice?
2   What is the most empathic thing you can think of to say (regardless of whether you would actually say it or not)?

Take a moment to write your answers down before turning to Appendix 5 for the rest of this exercise (see also Shemmings 2011).

So how does this link to critical analysis? In two main ways – first, a lack of empathy impairs a social worker's ability to gather information, which in turn will make critical analysis more difficult; and second, a lack of analysis can also lead to a lack of empathy.

As noted above, Forrester et al. found that a lack of empathy led to higher resistance and lower levels of information sharing by the parent. A low empathy response to the scenario in Exercise 6 would be something like: 'Could you show me the medicine bottle, so I can check the side-effects?'. The implication of such a response is that you do not believe the mother's account – you are asking her to prove what she says is true. Many will no doubt be thinking that some parents do lie to social workers, more if we include withholding information as a form of lying, and indeed we know this to be the case from various Serious Case Reviews of children who have died or been seriously injured.

Many may also be thinking that it is important to challenge parents and to examine what they tell us rather than just accept things at face value and again, we know that there are risks when social workers feel unable to challenge parents. However, the point we are making is that challenging parents and empathic communication are *not* mutually exclusive; you can 'do' both of them at the same time. Of course, the social worker in this scenario does need to find out if the parent's account of experiencing side effects is a plausible one but an immediate, acerbic response, lacking in empathy, will lead only to greater resistance and lower levels of information sharing, surely an outcome that would not be conducive to lowering any risk for the child.

Therefore, even if you did feel the parent was lying or just felt that you needed to 'check out' what you were being told, it would still not make sense to communicate in such a way as to indicate a low level of empathy. Without greater information from the parent, you will be at a disadvantage when trying to think analytically about any possible risk to the child.

The second link between empathy and critical analysis – that a lack of critical analysis can lead to lower levels of empathic communication – is also important and works in two ways. First, being analytical about your own communication skills can enable you to more clearly understand how you are likely to 'be experienced' by service users. Here, we are talking about analysis in the sense of thinking about and reflecting upon how emotional states are linked with behaviour (Fonagy et al. 1991). If your communication style results in service users feeling angry, mistrusted and marginalized, then they are likely to respond negatively to you. In other words, thinking analytically about communication can help you reflect on how the way you communicate is impacting on services users and on what you are trying to achieve.

However, the relationship also appears to us to work the other way as well. As we set out above, being able to think in terms of abductive reasoning or hypothesizing is important in developing an analytical mindset. If your sole hypothesis in Exercise 6 is that the parent is lying about their medication, then your response will probably be limited to finding out if the medication they are taking does produce these types of side effects. If you are able to think of at least one more hypothesis, then perhaps you will not so readily believe the parent must be lying.

Communicating in person

So, we have seen that empathy is a key factor in good (interpersonal) communication but it is not the only factor. Practitioners are often required to communicate in person with service users, other professionals and colleagues and communicating with people directly can be a messy, complicated business, especially when discussing issues such as mental ill health, loss of independence, risk to children and so on. Practitioners can often feel immobilized in their communication because of the emotional intensity of the situation (Walker 2008). Keeping an analytical mindset when faced with trauma, distress, despair and anger is far from easy.

A key idea that we would like to explore is that of rupture and repair, an idea taken from attachment theory. The idea of two people being 'attuned' in their communication is important and refers to the feeling of two people being in emotionally similar states such as that they feel 'in sync' – communication tends to feel easy when you achieve attunement. Rupture describes what occurs when two people fall out of attunement (or fail to achieve it). Fosha (2003) gives the example of a mother playing with a baby. A mother and baby can be said to be attuned when the mother claps her hands and expresses happiness and this is followed by the infant clapping and looking happy as well. However, if the infant becomes over-stimulated by this, they may look away from the mother so as to lower the stimulation. This act of looking away is a rupture; for a brief moment, the infant will be in a serious mood, not happy as before, while the mother remains in a state of happiness. This type of rupture occurs frequently in all close relationships (Fonagy and Target 2001) and as such, is relatively insignificant. What can be more significant is how ruptures are repaired. In Fosha's example, the mother quickly notices the infant's reticence to continue the game and stops clapping. The infant then makes eye contact again and thus the rupture is repaired. These 'attunement-rupture-repair-attunement' sequences are thought to be important in helping infants regulate their own emotions. However, as Walker notes, prolonged ruptures can lead to awkward feelings such as protest or even fear and shame.

How does this relate to communication between practitioners and service users? The link we would highlight is the importance of repairing ruptures in communication, especially in situations of heightened emotions. Freezing up in the face of distress, trauma or anger will prolong the rupture and make the repair much more difficult, if it occurs at all. Being able to analyse one's own responses to situations of rupture, being conscious of them and planning what to do when they occur, should in our view be a required part of social work training and education.

Clarity in written communication

Clear communication, both interpersonal and written, often follows from clear thinking. Clear thinking is often best expressed in clear communication. Unfortunately, there is a tendency in social work to slip into the use of jargon. Depending on your field of practice, you may know what the following mean: POVA, ICPC, t/c, RAP, CP, EBD and AD.[1] Or you may not! However, although these are obvious examples of jargon, practitioners can easily slip into using jargon without realizing it.

> **Reflection point: do you use jargon?**
>
> Here are some common terms in social work and how they were interpreted by a group of service users on behalf of the Social Care Institute for Excellence.
>
> Voluntary agencies – people with no experience
> Maintain – thought to be related to child maintenance
> Sensitive – something sore and tender
> Encompass – a way of finding directions
> Agencies – second hand clothes shops
> Common (values) – cheap and nasty
> Eligibility – a good catch for marriage
> Allocation process – related to getting a new house
> Function – a wedding, party or funeral
> Gender – most did not know what this might mean
> Networks – no one knew this word
>
> As you can see, what might seem to be 'straightforward' words (to practitioners) can actually be very confusing for some service users.

However, even if jargon is avoided, there can also be a tendency for reports to be written in overly complicated language. The Social Work Inspection Agency in Scotland reviewed over 1000 social work reports and found 'the language used was . . . often over complicated and insufficiently clear' (2010: 75). Often this appears to be unintentional. At other times, there is sense that perhaps the report is being written in a more complicated way than necessary in order that it perhaps sounds more important or more insightful than would otherwise be the case.

Practice example: using clear written language

Imagine the following scenario (provided by Professor Shemmings). You complete an assessment regarding Tommy, a child exhibiting some aggressive behaviour at nursery. The nursery have referred Tommy for an assessment as they are worried about what might be happening at home and about the affects of his behaviour on his success at the nursery. After doing some home and school visits, you conclude your assessment as follows:

> *Tommy is exhibiting some challenging behaviour in the nursery and this is a concern. This had led to Tommy being isolated from his peer group and he is not progressing academically or socially as he should. At home, I have observed that Tommy's parents are often insensitive towards him and it is my assessment that this is largely responsible for Tommy's behaviour in the nursery. I would recommend that Tommy's parents need to gain a greater insight into Tommy and how their parenting of him affects him.*

This may seem relatively clear but we would invite you to contrast it with the following:

> *I am worried about Tommy because of the way he behaves and shows his feelings, how this affects his confidence and makes it difficult for him to make friends. Tommy is violent at nursery and he is not learning as fast as his ability suggests he can. At home, Tommy often feels unwanted by his parents and they can say harsh things about him. I am worried that I have never heard Tommy's parents say anything kind to him or about him. I believe that Tommy feels unloved by his parents and as a result, he shows his feelings through his behaviour at the nursery and also at home. Tommy's parents need help to feel more affectionate towards him and show Tommy how they feel by telling him and spending time with him. They also need help to understand what this must all be like for Tommy.*

Although the second example is longer (147 versus 87 words), we believe it is also much clearer, while saying the same things. Actually, we believe that it says more – the links between Tommy's behaviour at nursery and his experiences at home are clearer in the second example, precisely because of the more straightforward language. Rather than simply saying the parenting is 'insensitive', the second example makes it clear that Tommy experiences this via negative language and a lack of affection. It may be that if you are struggling to write down or explain your thoughts in an easy to understand way, this could be a reflection of a lack of clarity in your thinking, rather than a deficit in your writing ability.

Exercise 8   Keep it simple

The aim of this exercise is to re-write the following excerpts from reports and assessments into as clear language as possible. Remember, the aim is to demonstrate the clarity of your thinking by using clear language. A secondary aim is to keep what you write as brief as possible, but do not sacrifice clarity for the sake of brevity.

Task: Re-write the following two paragraphs, aiming for (1) clarity and (2) brevity (you should feel free to speculate as required in order to re-write the paragraphs more clearly).

(1) I visited Mr Cooke at home and interviewed him about his daily life. Mr Cooke informed me that he feels his self-care skills are reasonably good; Mr Cooke feels he is able to meet his own needs for nutrition, for personal care and for stimulation at home. In terms of social relationships, Mr Cooke is part of various networks including a local mosque. However, I had the impression from interviewing Mr Cooke that he showed some evidence of short-term memory loss and this was non-commensurate for a man of his age. On observation, the home environment was reasonably clean and tidy – however, I did notice several areas of concern, including a poorly maintained aquarium. With his consent, I spoke with Mr Cooke's GP who informed me that he regularly visits Mr Cooke at home and finds him to be often confused and disoriented.

(2) Mrs Shah has been admitted to her local mental health hospital following an attempted suicide. Mrs Shah is in the hospital via a voluntary admission. Mrs Shah has presented with some depressive behaviour on the ward. Mrs Shah often makes statements that could be considered examples of suicidal ideation. Mrs Shah informs that she does not feel her life is worth living. While on the ward, I am aware that Mrs Shah has been visited by members of her extended family network, namely her nephew. These visits seem to have a positive impact on Mrs Shah's self-esteem and her presentation in periods shortly after these visits is also improved. Mrs Shah likely requires an extended in-patient admission if her risk-profile in future is to be improved.

You can see an example of how we completed this exercise in Appendix 6.

Reflection

The final skill we wish to discuss is that of reflection. The report of the Social Work Reform Board and the Munro report into child protection both set out the need for reflective social work practice. According to Munro, 'Our intuitive capacity is vast, swift and largely unconscious. "Reflective practice" is the time and effort spent to pull out one's intuitive reasoning so that it can be reviewed and communicated' (2009: 2). Reflective practice is not about 'overcoming' our intuitive judgements and biases – as we discussed in an earlier chapter, this is not possible. Rather, reflection is the process by which we can learn about our biases, about how they might be impacting on our thinking and learning to account for them. It is hard to recognize our own intuitive biases because they feel so obvious to us. When we reflect on them, the result can be that we find it easier to think about all of the reasons why our own view is correct and more difficult to think of reasons why we might be wrong.

Given this difficulty, how can we use reflection in an effective way? There are various models of reflection ranging from the relatively simple (e.g. Rolfe et al. 2001; see Fig. 2.2) to the relatively complex (e.g. Gibbs 1988). Most of the models take a similar approach to that of Rolfe et al. although they may expand on particular parts of the model. At the heart of any reflective practice is the ability to identify what (you are thinking), to question it (so what) and then to think about what to do next.

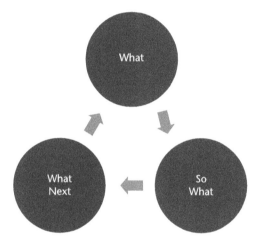

Figure 2.2   Rolfe et al.'s (2001) model of reflective practice

---

Exercise 9   Reflection in practice

This exercise will help you apply Rolfe et al.'s model of reflection to a case study.

You are a social worker in an older persons' team. You receive a call from Joan, daughter of 70-year-old Mrs Bee. Joan reports that she can no longer manage to care for her mother safely at home and asks about residential care. You visit Mrs Bee the next day and find her home alone (she tells you Joan has gone to the shops). Mrs Bee easily enters into conversation and if anything, is over friendly. She describes all the things she does, such as visiting friends and her son. Mrs Bee makes you a cup of tea and you continue to talk. After a while, you notice that Mrs Bee's stories are somewhat repetitive and some of the details are quite vague. Joan then returns from shopping and you notice a distinct 'cooling' in the atmosphere. Joan and Mrs Bee start disagreeing about what she can and cannot do for herself but both of them sound reasonable and coherent to you. Joan says her mother needs supervision, especially when she goes out, and tells you about a time she found her offering money to a stranger in a betting shop. Mrs Bee becomes annoyed and accuses Joan of trying to get rid of her.

1   How would you describe 'what' is happening in the case study above? What are your initial 'gut' or intuitive feelings about what is going on?
2   Once you are clear on the 'what', can you now say 'so what'? In other words, given what you think is going on, what is the significance of it?
3   What would you do next? What do you think Joan and Mrs Bee might do next?

You can see an example of how we completed this exercise in Appendix 7.

Depending on how you completed Exercise 8 – whether on your own or in a small group – you may have found it easier or harder. If so, this illustrates a key point about reflective practice: it is often much easier to engage in constructive reflection in combination with others. This is because it is often easier to see the contradictions, oversights and biases in someone else's intuitive reasoning than in your own. Finding a trusted colleague with which to engage in reflection together is so important for practice and this is partly why supervision is often the key dynamic (see Chapter 7).

Developing your skills

As noted in the Introduction, it is very difficult to learn skills from a book and although we have outlined the skills we think are important for critical analysis and discussed some possible ways of assessing your own proficiency, we would not claim that simply reading this chapter or even the whole book is enough to learn these skills. Our purpose has been to set out the skills we think you should focus on in order to develop an analytical mindset. In the recommended reading/resources section below, we have included a number of places where you can find out more information about these skills and how you might go about developing and practising them.

Summary and conclusions

In this chapter we have covered quite a lot of material. We have highlighted five key skills that we believe form the bedrock of being analytically minded. Where possible, we have included exercises to help you rate your own level of competence in each of these areas and we have also pointed out that skills require practice. We have also argued that in many cases, the relationship between these five skills and critical analysis is bi-directional, with improvements in the skills leading to improvements in critical analysis, which in turn will lead to improvements in the skills.

One final piece of advice – if you want to learn how to do anything well, it can be tempting to break it down into smaller parts and practise each part until you become really good at it. For example, if you want to become really good at tennis, you might decide to focus just on your serve and spend hours serving over and over again. However, the best approach is actually to practise everything at the same time, an approach known as 'interleaving'. That is, in order to become a better tennis player, you should spend time on serving, backhands, volleys, overhead smashes and your footwork all within the same session. The overall goal must be consistent – in this case, becoming really good at tennis – but as long as the skills all relate, mixing them up is a better way to learn and become good at them than practising them individually. This translates to the aim of becoming analytically minded as follows: if you are going to practise the related skills, it is better to try and learn them all together, interleaving them, rather than focus on, say, time management and then communication and then reflection and so on. For example, it would be better to engage in some reflective discussion with a colleague and then write a short report about what you have learned within a deadline – this way, you are practising all three together.

Key points from this chapter include

- Critical analysis is a skill and a skill must be practised.
- Five key skills contribute towards the skill of critical analysis – time management, abductive reasoning, research-mindedness, communication and reflection.
- Becoming analytically minded is not something you can simply decide to do, it is something that requires patience, practice and hard work.

Recommended reading/resources

Time management

'Mind Tools' website – 'how to' website for learning practical skills such as time management, stress management and communication. Many of the tools are available free of charge. (http://www.mindtools.com)

Research-mindedness

Orme, J. and Shemmings, D. (2010) *Developing Research Based Social Work Practice*. Basingstoke: Palgrave Macmillan.
Research Mindedness in Social Work and Social Care (SCIE) (http://www.resmind.swap.ac.uk/index.htm)

Communication

Communication skills for social workers (SCIE) – contains e-learning resources, available free of charge. (http://www.scie.org.uk/publications/elearning/communicationskills/index.asp)

Shemmings, D. (2011) What social workers need to know about empathy, *Community Care*. http://www.communitycare.co.uk/Articles/31/10/2011/117682/empathy-and-neuroscience-powerful-tools-for-social-workers.htm

Reflection

Smith, M.K. (2001, 2011) Donald Schön: learning, reflection and change, *The Encyclopedia of Informal Education*. www.infed.org/thinkers/et-schon.htm

3   Emotion and intuition

Chapter overview

In this chapter we explore:

- The role of emotions in intense and in everyday decision-making
- The importance of reflecting on emotional and intuitive reactions to practice
- How strong and unprocessed emotional reactions can compromise decision-making

---

Introduction

In this chapter we will recap some of the material on emotion and intuition that we discussed in the Introduction but will go into more detail. Critical analysis may typically be thought of as the application of reason and logic and as such, leaves little room for emotional responses or intuitive information. But as we have already said, our view of critical analysis in the context of social work is that this is both unrealistic and unhelpful. It is unrealistic because as Turney (2009) has pointed out, the emotional impact of difficult situations on professionals is profound and unless this impact is ameliorated (primarily via supervision – see Chapter 7) and actually harnessed, it will present a significant barrier to achieving a good level of critical analysis in your practice. It is unhelpful because properly understood and placed into context, our emotional and intuitive reactions can be a useful aid to our work.

In part, the role of emotion and intuition in critical analysis has been overlooked because of an imperative to base assessments and practice on 'evidence'. Unfortunately, this has resulted in some practitioners taking a mistaken view of what 'evidence-based practice' means, defining it as something like 'as I cannot prove (beyond reasonable doubt?) that this child is being abused, I cannot take any further action' or something similar (this is a view we have heard expressed in many different training events and situations). Please do not misunderstand our point – we do not believe that service users should be subject to statutory intervention based on practitioners' 'gut feelings' but at the same time, we need to be mindful that we do not end up using a lack of what might be called 'hard evidence' as an excuse to close case-work and to not offer support and help in non-statutory ways. Our argument is simply that emotion and intuition are an integral part of guiding your practice but that this needs to be done carefully and explicitly.

The other reason that emotion and intuition have been overlooked as playing a role in critical analysis is because of the way analysis is typically described in official guidance. As we have already pointed out, much official guidance for practitioners says that analysis is a separate part of the process of assessment, and therefore usually practised in front of a computer by an individual practitioner. This view of analysis encourages you to overlook the importance of intuition and of emotional reactions to service users because it encourages you to take account of only information that you can write into an assessment template. Dijksterhuis (2004) found that unconscious or intuitive thought could be superior to formal or conscious thought in certain situations, especially when the task being addressed involves highly complex information and lots of it. Dijksterhuis argued that this is because the conscious system of thought is biased towards more easily articulated information.

In addition, completing your analysis based only on formal (or conscious) reasoning, especially when this is undertaken solely in the office environment, is an exclusionary and disempowering approach – how can service users be involved in the analysis of their own circumstances if their role is to passively provide information for you, the practitioner, to take away and analyse? Of course, this could apply whenever analysis is undertaken as a separate, final stage in an assessment process but nevertheless, the sense of exclusion is, we feel, heightened if the service user's emotional and intuitive reactions, as well as those of the practitioner, are thought somehow irrelevant to the process.

When we talk about including emotional and intuitive reactions in your critical analysis, we would not expect practitioners to be writing things such as 'this service user makes me feel deeply uncomfortable' in their reports. Nevertheless, if you did feel like this, it would helpful to discuss it in supervision (see Chapter 7). Family therapists offer a good model for us here. If such a therapist were to find a client's apparent lack of willingness to take responsibility for their own behaviour frustrating and anger provoking, a good therapist would not seek to hide or ignore these emotions – after all, they are genuine and present in the relationship – but would seek to address them and to talk with the service user, even, about them. We strongly believe that social workers need to be just as comfortable in naming and discussing their emotional reactions. We would be worried to hear that a practitioner were not experiencing *any* emotional reactions to the kinds of situations social workers routinely encounter, such as child abuse, an elderly parent being forced out of their own home or a service user becoming overwhelmed by the symptoms of their mental ill health. So these emotional reactions are part of the role and hence need to be accounted for.

The role of emotion in decision-making

Many of you will be familiar with the character of Mr Spock from *Star Trek*. For any readers who are unfamiliar, Mr Spock is a hybrid alien-human, with a Vulcan father and a human mother. In the *Star Trek* universe, the Vulcan people value logic above all else and although Vulcans are born with emotional reactions, similar to – if not stronger than – humans, they train over many years to repress their emotional reactions and strive to make their decisions based purely on logic. Logic has such value to the Vulcan people that in the 2009 *Star Trek* file, when Mr Spock asks his father why he married his mother, he replies that 'marrying your mother was logical' (he later informs Spock that he actually married for love). To many people, this ideal – of being purely logical, purely rational – is almost something to aspire to, especially in a work or professional context. However, it is interesting to look at an extreme example, like Mr Spock, and consider how he might actually go about making a decision. When you consider the implications of being purely logical and rational more closely, it turns out that Mr Spock would have great difficulty in making any kind of decision at all, let alone a good one.

As LeDoux (1996) points out, making decisions without any reference to intuition is unlikely to be very successful. Imagine you are walking along a woodland path. You are perhaps deep in thought about something or other when suddenly, out of the corner of your eye, you see a thin, shadowy shape and it appears to be moving towards you. In a split second, an unconscious and intuitive part of your brain kicks in and you jump back. Now, the conscious part of your brain takes over and you notice, with some relief, that you have just jumped back from a stick moving slightly in the wind. You may feel a bit silly and be grateful no one is around to see you but on the other hand, if it had been a snake, you would have just had a lucky escape.

The difficulty for Mr Spock is that he would have trained himself, over many years, to prevent the intuitive reaction of jumping backwards and so, if Mr Spock were unlucky enough to live in a place with many poisonous snakes, he would probably not have lasted very long. Logically contemplating every potential snake in the woods is not likely to be a very successful survival strategy. But what does this have to do with everyday decision-making? Surely, in less extreme circumstances than (potentially) encountering poisonous snakes, the role of emotion or intuition is much reduced?

Not necessarily, according to Damasio (1994). Indeed, everyday decisions – such as whether to get up as soon as the alarm clock rings or not, choosing a seat on a crowded train or bus or whether to have honey or jam on your toast – all involve a degree of emotion, even if it does not feel like it. They do so via so-called gut feelings – emotional (and intuitive) bodily reactions. In these types of everyday decisions, your emotional mind will probably not 'force itself' into consciousness in quite the same way in our example above, but nevertheless, it is still there, quietly guiding the decision-making process in such a way that to describe your decisions as being just about rationality or logic is simply not accurate.

Evidence for this can be seen in the example of adults who have suffered damage to the frontal lobe of their brain. The frontal lobe, particularly an area known as the VMPFC (or ventromedial prefrontal cortex), plays a key role in the expression and experiencing of emotions (Greene 2007; Moll and de Oliveira-Souza 2007). Damage to this area leads to difficulties with planning and organizing behaviour (making decisions). This led Damasio (1991) to argue that when your ability to express and experience emotions is compromised so is your ability to make even quite simple decisions. This supports the idea that emotional reactions and responses are a key factor in all kinds of behaviour. In the next section we will look at an example of how emotional reactions can not only influence our decision-making but actually overwhelm it.

Hot cognition

The idea of 'hot cognition' is an important one when thinking about the importance of emotional reactions in highly charged situations. Hot cognition describes a phenomenon in which people make decisions while in highly aroused (emotional) states, when they are extremely attentive to their environment and highly aware of information around them (Ajzen 1991).

In various studies of doctors and surgeons, Roger Kneebone has found that by using simulations to practise their skills, these medical professionals could learn to make better decisions by becoming more used to dealing with strong emotional reactions. For example, in various studies of doctors and surgeons, Kneebone has found that some medics were making poor decisions without even being aware that they had done so. This was more likely to happen when the test subjects were placed in emotionally heightened situations. For example, imagine a scenario in which an emergency doctor is trying to treat an aggressive patient in a hospital A&E department. Perhaps the patient is disoriented as a result of drugs or alcohol. The patient might be making threats to the doctor as well as acting strangely and unpredictably. It might be late at night, at the end of a long and challenging shift. The doctor knows that all she needs to do is complete a series of simple medical procedures, such as checking the patient's blood pressure. That is, when the situation is calm and when the doctor is well rested, these are simple procedures but in the situation described here, it may not be surprising to think that the doctor could become overwhelmed and start to misread the results of the tests or misadminister them. However, what Kneebone's research suggests is not only does this happen but that the professional may not be aware of their poor performance.

What this tells us is that in highly conflicted and emotionally arousing situations, not only is our ability to perform our job impaired but also our self-reflective ability to know that we have not performed our job very well is also impaired. This has significance for practitioners in a range of social care and health settings. Imagine (or recall) the emotional pressure of responding to parents who you know have abused their child, parents who are shouting at you, accusing you of lying, of trying to take their child from them. Or service users with severe mental health difficulties, accusing you of working against them, of trying to drug them, trying to separate them from their families and deprive them of their liberty. Or an elderly service user with severe dementia, who is confused, frightened, angry and upset. All of these situations and more are at least the equivalent of the trainee doctors trying to administer relatively simple medical procedures to an angry and aggressive patient.

Given the above, how can we manage such emotional arousal and still think clearly and analytically about our practice? First, the good news. Practice is an effective way of compensating for the effects of hot cognition. As we will discuss in more detail in Chapter 7, supervision can be our 'safe space' in which to talk about the potentially difficult and emotionally challenging situations we can face, how they make us feel and perhaps even more importantly, to practise, *to literally act out*, what we are going to do, say and how the service user might respond or act during the encounter. Clearly, there are many unforeseen things that can occur in day-to-day practise, which can create significant and unexpected emotional reactions – this is simply unavoidable. Nevertheless, explicitly practising with supervisors and colleagues how best to effectively manage and interact with angry and possibly aggressive service users is likely to be one of the best ways to ensure that, when the unexpected does occur, you will have a series of techniques and ideas to rely on. In addition to using supervision, another approach is to use the types of training materials currently being produced by the University of Kent (Shemmings and Reeves 2012).

The role of intuition in decision-making

In the Introduction, we explored four key psychological qualities that affect how people think. We examined the role of values and beliefs, intuition and conscious thought, narratives and confirmation bias. In Chapter 1, we discussed in some more detail the role of formal and intuitive thinking. We are going to develop these ideas further here before presenting an exercise.

It is often believed that experts are more able to use intuition than novices because of their greater degree of knowledge and experience when compared with beginners. In other words, because an expert is likely to have experienced a similar situation before, they can use their intuition as a short cut to making good decisions. However, this is not always the case. For practical problems that need to be solved, it can be the other way around. Pretz (2008) studied the role of intuition and formal analysis and considered how undergraduates of differing degrees of experience approached the problems of college life. Pretz considered such practical problems as how to maintain friendships and how to deal with a roommate who is suspected of 'stealing' (e.g. taking shared food items and not replacing them). Pretz's sample was divided into first year, second year, third year and fourth year undergraduates. Pretz found that the more experienced undergraduates – the fourth year students – were able to find better solutions to these types of problems when they used formal or reasoned analysis, whereas the least experienced undergraduates – the first year students – did better when they used a more intuitive approach. This indicated to Pretz that once you have a level of expertise and experience (as with the fourth year undergraduates) you are in a better position to use formal analysis but when you lack expertise and experience, it can be better to use intuition, at least when dealing with practical problems.

In many ways, this study is a challenge to the 'common sense' view of intuition. Are we to conclude that those lacking in expertise and experience, perhaps newly qualified practitioners, would be better off if they simply trusted their intuitions? Clearly, this could be a risky and potentially discriminatory approach to take. Nevertheless, it cannot be denied that many of the issues that practitioners face are of a practical nature.

However, there is an added complication. When an intuitive approach yields a good outcome – a child is kept safe, a service user is helped to stop misusing substances or a service user with learning difficulties is supported to live independently in the community – it is unlikely that anyone will question the decision-making process that led to such an outcome. If, on the other hand, the outcomes are negative, then important questions may be asked as to what led up to the negative outcome, either in a formal way, such as with a Serious Case Review, or less formally, via a management or 'in-house' case review (see Lamond and Thompson 2000). This should not lead to the conclusion that intuition should form no part of the analytical and decision-making process but what it does mean is that the role of intuition has to be made explicit and transparent to service users and managers. But how can this be done when intuition is variously described as 'understanding without rationale' (Benner and Tanner 1987: 3), 'knowledge independent of the linear reasoning process' (Rew and Barron 1987: 60) and as something which is 'not . . . able to be explained in a tangible manner' (Cioffi 1997: 204, taken from Lamond and Thompson 2000)?

Our view is that it is not the *use* of intuition that is of concern but the use of intuition *un-reflected upon*. As we discussed in Chapter 2, the skill of reflection is crucial for critical analysis. Using the simple model of reflection that we presented on page 43, you could imagine (or recall) a particular home visit which left you feeling uneasy or unsettled. Using the model of reflection on page 43 would be one way of prompting you to consider 'so what?'. By asking this question explicitly, you will help to ensure that your feelings are not overlooked but also that they do not become, on their own, the basis for taking specific actions that may be unreasonable or unfair or unhelpful for the service user.

Exercise 10 will seek to demonstrate the role that emotion and intuition can have in practice. Clearly, reading about a scenario will not generate nearly the same emotional or intuitive reaction as actually partaking in a real-life situation. However, we would invite you to, as far as possible, 'inhabit' the scenario and imagine yourself physically in the scenario as described. This exercise is based on the serious game, *Rosie*, produced by the Child Protection Centre, University of Kent and is included with the kind permission of Professor David Shemmings.

Exercise 10   The role of emotion and intuition in practice

In this scenario, imagine you are a female child protection social worker. You are asked by your manager to complete an assessment of a 4-year-old named Rosie. Her nursery, who report that recently she has started to appear very nervous or even scared about visiting the toilet, has referred Rosie to your agency. Rosie has also drawn a picture of a man with a large snake coming out of his trousers.

Reflection point: intuitive thoughts, values and beliefs

Already, your intuitions and your values and beliefs will be influencing how you feel and think about even this brief amount of information.

For example, if you hold a core value that family life is private and only under extreme circumstances should the state intervene, you may already be questioning whether your agency should even have accepted such a referral.

You may also have an intuitive fear of snakes – many people do – and this may be influencing your reaction to what Rosie has drawn. You may also intuitively thinking of the snake as

a phallic object. Consider whether you may have felt differently if Rosie had drawn a picture of a man with a lizard or rat coming out of his trousers.

You go to visit Rosie at home and are greeted by an overweight, white male, who appears unkempt in appearance. He appears to be leering at you and makes suggestive comments about going on a date with you. You negotiate your way inside and meet Rosie's mother. You also see an older male child playing a violent computer game in the bedroom. Rosie's mother informs you that Rosie is at nursery and another baby is asleep upstairs. You start to ask Rosie's mother what she knows about the referral from the nursery. The man who let you in stands very close to you and starts to speak more loudly, telling you this is all a waste of time and asking why you are poking around.

Reflection point: intuitive thoughts

Imagine how you might feel as a lone female worker in an unfamiliar house with an intimidating man. Your intuition will almost certainty be 'suggesting' to you that you should leave. However, even though most practitioners would not actually leave, as we saw with the idea of hot cognition, strong emotional reactions can influence conscious decision-making.

You manage to defuse the situation by asking for a cup of tea, which the man goes off to make for you. As you speak further with Rosie's mother, she tells you that the man, Danny, owns a snake and this must be why Rosie drew the picture. Rosie's mother says that Danny is not Rosie's father but he is a really caring man and always helps give her a bath and put her to bed. After this, you end the visit and say you will be in contact again soon.

Reflection point: narratives and confirmation bias

What potential narratives might you, the social worker, Danny and Rosie's mother hold about what has happened so far? In other words, what story might each person be telling themselves and others about the events leading from the nursery's referral?

Task: Generate a hypothesis about this situation, based on the intuitive and reflective re-actions you have noted. Once you have a hypothesis, think about what information would disprove or disconfirm it.

Summary and conclusions

In summary, we have argued that emotional and intuitive processes will inevitably play a part in your thinking. Therefore, it is not a question as to *whether* they should have a role but *how to get the best out of them*. We have shown an example of how intense emotional reactions – such as hot cognition – can lead to poor decision-making and can even mislead practitioners into believing they have done things when they have not. This leads to the conclusion that supervision and the skill of reflection, as discussed in Chapter 2, are key components in critical analysis.

Key points from this chapter include

- It is important to consider how service users can be included in an analysis of their own situation, and not viewed simply as providers of information to be analysed by others.
- Preparation and practice are vital in dealing appropriately with highly charged and emotional situations.
- Reflection plays a crucial role in ensuring that intuitive and emotional reactions are consciously included in the analytical process but without becoming the source of biased or prejudicial decision-making.

Recommended reading

Howe, D. (2008) *The Emotionally Intelligent Social Worker.* Basingstoke: Palgrave Macmillan.

4 Approaches to analysis

Chapter overview

By the end of this chapter, you should:

- Understand three approaches to analysis – strengths, weaknesses, opportunities and threats (SWOT), a basic systemic approach and an ecological-transactional approach
- Understand the types of cases in which the three models may be applied
- Be able to reflect on the limitations of applying each of the three models in practice
- Have had an opportunity to apply each of the approaches to a case example

Introduction

In this chapter, we will introduce three approaches to critical analysis in practice. The sections in this chapter are as follows: strengths, weaknesses, opportunities and threats (SWOT), basic systemic approach and an ecological-transactional approach. All of these approaches are suitable for assessing need and risk in the course of practice. We then include a more philosophical section on risk and on the different ways practitioners may approach this topic. As outlined in the Introduction, it is not our intention that practitioners should apply these three models in a 'rigid' or formulaic way; rather you will be able to adapt them for your own practice. In addition, these models can be used to practise your analytical skills and help develop a more analytical mindset. As with any model, there are strengths and weaknesses to each of them and our aim is to enable you to develop an understanding of the concepts of each model and give you the knowledge to decide for yourselves how best they could be used. Starting with SWOT in the next section, the models presented in this chapter are sequentially more complicated. Each of these is more complex than the last and we chose these specific approaches by design, to enable you to think about and practise a basic, intermediate and then more complex level of critical analysis.

Strengths, weaknesses, opportunities and threats (SWOT)

The SWOT model originated in the United States of America, primarily as a tool for businesses to plan strategy and future direction. However, it has also been applied to large non-business agencies as well. For example, Westhues et al. (2001) used SWOT to analyse the Canadian social work profession as a whole. It can also be useful for individuals in thinking about, for example, their job prospects and future career goals. Pearce (2007) suggested that one of the best things about SWOT is that it can enable individuals to reflect on their own experiences (of work) and help to identify areas where they might be able to make improvements. However, our intention is to adapt SWOT for use with service users and their families. In doing so, we will draw on the work of Dalzell and Sawyer (2011), who wrote about the application of SWOT to team and group environments.

Applying SWOT to social work practice

A simple way to apply SWOT in practice is to construct a four-section framework listing the strengths, weaknesses, opportunities and threats related to the service user (see Fig. 4.1). However, we have made some changes to the wording of the model, in order to better reflect the underlying values of the social work profession, replacing 'threats' with 'risks' (or 'needs') and 'weaknesses' with 'challenges'. This results in a reformulated SCOR model (see Dalzell and Sawyer 2011: 108). The simplicity of this tool makes it ideal as a basic model for critical analysis. It offers a relatively easy way of organizing information and is so simple that it could be quite easily used in conjunction with or alongside the service user. We will go through each heading in turn and suggest how you might use one to organize the information you might have.

Risks or needs: This heading would include any child or adult protection issues, such as the impact of substance misuse, violence in the home or financial abuse. However, this section should also be used to identify unmet needs, which may not be 'risky' in the sense of potentially causing harm but nevertheless would need to be addressed in order to ensure or maximize the well being of the service user. Rather than simply list a series of risks or needs, we would encourage you to include a consideration of the actual or

Strengths	Challenges
Opportunities	Risks (or needs)

Figure 4.1   An adapted strengths, weaknesses, opportunities and threats framework – a SCOR model.

potential consequences of each risk or unmet need. For example, in the case of a family who were not accessing all of their welfare benefits, you might consider how living on a low income over an extended period of time could result in concrete problems, such as having to choose whether to eat or to heat their home. In other words, we think the model will be most useful if you can learn to think about the (potential) impact of unmet needs or risks rather than just the needs or risks themselves.

Strengths: This heading would include the resources or support available to offset the risks or to meet the needs identified in the previous section. It is important to note that in the context of social work practice, a 'strength' is more than simply saying 'something nice' about the service user or their family. The following anecdote is an example of how *not* to think about strengths in this context – as a team manager, you read the assessment of a newly qualified social worker, who clearly identifies the risks to a young child from living with a man previously convicted of the sexual assault of a child. Under strengths, the social worker informs you that '[the man] is always welcoming and polite when I visit and often makes me a cup of tea'. In your role as manager, you may wonder why this has been included. Often, social workers feel that they need to find at least one 'strength' (or 'nice thing') to say about a family or service user they are working with. It is our view that this is the wrong way to think about strengths in social work practice. Rather, a strength must be something that offsets a risk or helps meet a need (or has the potential to do so). For example, for the family not claiming all of their benefit entitlements, a strength might be that a friend or a member of the wider family is providing regular cash payments to help buy food or that one of the adults in the family has recently started working for a few hours a week. The money provided as a result would be a strength because it would be offsetting the risk of the family not being able to afford everyday essentials as a result of not claiming all of their benefit entitlements. This strength could mean the family are avoiding a crisis and have enough time to make a full benefit claim before they find themselves unable to afford the things they need.

Opportunities: This heading would include a consideration of existing but unexplored possibilities for the service user, within their family, their social network or the community. In the case of the family not claiming all of their benefit entitlements, it may be that they have a friend who could help them attend the Job Centre and complete an application form for an unclaimed benefit. Being aware of simple avenues of support, such as a friend or family member who could help, and being able to draw on these kinds of 'resources', is a perfectly good example of what good social work practice is all about.

Challenges: This heading would include a consideration of any issues that might impair or complicate the ability of services or the service user and their family to address the risks and unmet needs identified. These challenges may relate to the service user or the family or they may be external. For example, a challenge for the family not accessing all of their benefit entitlements may be that their job(s) are insecure and there is a high chance they will be unemployed in the near future.

We hope that you can see how SWOT can be used as a very simple way of organizing information and making more explicit the links between information in each of the four areas. SWOT also offers a helpful visual representation of areas in which perhaps you have a lot of information and areas where you have much less. For example, having organized the information you have about a particular service user, you might find you have lots of information about risks or needs but very little about strengths. A visual representation can also be helpful for service users, as it can make your assessment much clearer for them to understand and make it easier for them to contribute.

Limitations of SWOT

One of the limitations of our modified SWOT approach is that it could result in an over-simplification of a complex situation. Although we have previously advised on the need not to overcomplicate simple issues, it is just as important to recognize the importance of not oversimplifying either. In practice, many issues for service users can overlap and what is a strength in one context or at one time might prove to be a risk in another context or at a different time. This would not invalidate the model but would require you to keep it up to date. Furthermore, there is only limited research regarding the application of SWOT to practise in this way. Ghazinoory et al. 2011 reviewed the body of research regarding the application of SWOT and made no mention of applications in social work or social care although they did find considerable applications in 'health or health care', which overlap with social care. The limited evidence about the efficacy of SWOT in social work practice means that it is difficult to specify the kinds of cases or families in which it can be most usefully applied.

Practice example: using SWOT

A social worker in a disabled children's team receives a referral for a 7-year-old girl with a severe learning disability. The referral from her school contains the following information:

Family details:

Evette lives with her biological mother and her stepfather, aged 23 and 30 respectively. Evette has no contact with her biological father. Evette's mother is unemployed and acts as a full-time carer for her children. Evette's stepfather is unemployed as well. Evette has two younger half-siblings. The family live in a deprived area of town in a two bedroom flat.

Referral information:

Evette often arrives at school in unkempt clothing and sometimes looks 'grubby'. Evette often seems hungry when she arrives. Evette's two half-siblings attend the school as well and they too can appear unkempt but do not seem hungry. Evette has attended the school for 18 months; prior to six months ago, she seemed to be doing okay. It is not clear what happened to cause the change although we think that her stepfather lost his job around this time. Both Evette's mother and stepfather come to the school with all of the children at various times and both attend parents' evenings.

As an example, Evette recently had an accident in the playground – she fell over – and her stepfather attended the school straight away. Evette seemed please to see him.

A SWOT (or 'SCOR') analysis could be completed as follows:

Strengths	Challenges
• Mother and stepfather engaged with school • Evette attends school regularly? • Evette seemed happy to see her stepfather	• No contact with birth father? • Stepfather out of work (not by choice?) • Family live in deprived area • May not be in suitable housing?
Opportunities	**Risks (or needs)**
• Until six months ago, things seemed to be going okay • Could birth father help in some way? Would need to know why there is no contact • Mother and stepfather may be willing to engage with other services (given that they engage with school)	• Children all appear 'grubby' at times • Evette sometimes appears hungry • Why do other children not appear hungry as well? Is Evette being 'singled out' by her family in some way?

From this relatively simple example, one can start to see how this basic approach to analysis can start to help in organizing information and in seeing how different elements may interrelate. It can also help highlight what information may be particularly valuable to gather in the actual assessment (remember, this example is based solely on the referral – a SWOT analysis following an assessment would be a lot more detailed). In this example, the social worker may wish to explore why birth father does not have contact why the other children do not appear hungry but Evette does, how come the family manage to get all the children to school regularly but not always clean and fed and what changed six months ago, the obvious suggestion being the loss of stepfather's job but the key would be to explore why and how (and if) this is a sufficient explanation for the change.

Basic systems approach

In this section, we discuss a basic systems approach, something which offers a more sophisticated model for critical analysis than our modified SWOT. A basic systems approach can encourage you to think more widely than the service user and their immediate family and to think about the service user as part of a wider 'system'. A simple example of a systemic approach can be outlined as follows:

> Imagine a service user with severe depression. The severity of their depression is such that they find it difficult to leave the house, difficult to have visitors and

difficult to look after themselves (to wash and eat and so on). A simple medical approach might be to treat the chemical imbalance in their brain with a pill. A systems approach would seek to understand how the person's depression is influenced by other people and factors around them. For example, perhaps the service user recently lost his job. Could helping the service user find some voluntary work help them regain a sense of purpose and, perhaps alongside medical treatment, ensure that their recovery from depression is more complete and more rounded than only using medical treatment?

This is only meant to be a very simply example but the underlying premise of this approach is that to effectively help service users, you need to understand the systems that they are a part of (see Pincus and Minahan 1973). This is because the interaction between different parts of a system can be significant for the service user. Such an approach also encourages you to think about your own place or role within the system, rather than viewing yourself as some kind of neutral agent.

Assumptions underpinning a systems approach

One of the key assumptions made by systems theory is that 'A system is a collection of parts . . . that interact to accomplish an overall goal. We therefore need to study it in terms of wholes and interactions, not taking the reductionist route of picking out individual components for study' (Munro and Hubbard 2011: 728). Accordingly, when applying a basic systems approach to practice, practitioners and service users should be treated as being part of something much bigger than themselves and not just as individual people having individual interactions. In other words, it is more helpful to think in this way than to think of service users as isolated individuals, with needs or risks isolated from their wider environment. Forder (1976) argued that systems themselves can exhibit certain characteristics such as openness, 'goal-orientation' and responsiveness to information. This means that different networks of people and organizations may be more or less open to outside help, they may share the same goals or have conflicting goals and they may be more or less open to new information and ideas.

Practice example: using a basic systems approach

Imagine you are working with a mother and her 7-week-old baby. The mother is originally from Estonia and moved to the UK around 12 months ago, since when she has been working part time for 'cash in hand'. The baby is diagnosed with Down Syndrome at birth but the mother does not attend several medical appointments. The mother does not register the birth of the baby or register the baby with a GP.

As the baby's social worker, you visit the baby at home and find that the small flat where they are living is very hot, the baby is wrapped tightly in many blankets and placed to sleep in a cot next to a radiator. This raises your concern about the risk of cot death. You discover from the baby's health visitor that the mother has been advised on many occasions about the risks of the baby getting too hot and yet she appears to make no changes.

It can be easy as a practitioner in such a situation to become frustrated with the mother, arguing that she has been given advice and just needs to follow it. However, a basic systems approach will encourage you to think more deeply about the meaning of advice from professionals for this mother, the importance of understanding the mother's previous experience of babies and children (if any) and so on.

As with all example vignettes, it may well be the case that there is insufficient information in this example to form a definitive conclusion. However, our intention here is only to demonstrate that thinking more broadly – systemically – about a service user can result in a better understanding of them, rather than viewing a service user as simply 'an individual' and, as in this example, potentially becoming frustrated with the mother for not 'choosing' to follow the 'simple advice' of professionals. According to Forder (1976), systems are 'open' when they frequently interact with, and provide and receive information to and from, other systems. In the example of the mother and baby above, does the mother have frequent contact with other new mothers and so have the opportunity to talk about things like registering babies, how warm a baby needs to be or is she more isolated and hence, has to rely just on her own intuition and knowledge?

Another example of how thinking systemically can help you obtain a deeper understanding can be seen in the frequent plot device used in soap operas of a third party, such as a child, finding out about a mother's extra-marital relationship before their father knows – such a scenario would be an example of how one part of a system (the child) can have access to information that another part (the father) remains oblivious to. Often, in soaps, a child in this position would be seen stressing and worrying about whether to tell their father, what his reaction might be and what it might do to his experience of family life. This neatly illustrates the power of information in systems.

Goal orientation refers to the 'inbuilt desire' of systems to achieve or maintain stability. This means that systems 'seek' to remain the same or consistent over time (see Forder 1976). Taking our example of the soap opera, this would suggest that part of the child's stress is caused by their understanding of the potentially explosive (soap language!) nature of the information they have; sharing the information with the father will surely cause the system of the family to change significantly.

However, because the child is also part of other systems, such as their school, the effects of this information will not necessarily be restricted to just the family. This could lead to the child acting out at school as a result of their worry and anxiety, perhaps resulting in a school counsellor becoming involved (and because we are talking about a soap opera, the school counsellor would inevitably be the person with whom the child's mother is having her extra-marital relationship).

Ultimately, systems theory tells us that what causes difficulties and challenges for service users is not necessarily related to anything personal or individual to them. Instead, it is the interactions between the personal and the individual and wider systems that are the key. Applying these ideas to practice, Pincus and Minahan (1973) suggest that a key role for practitioners is to help service users resolve difficulties in terms of their interactions with others rather than by focusing on individual change. Using practice examples, we will explore this a bit further.

Applying a basic systems approach to practice

A basic systems approach to practice should encourage practitioners to feel and act curiously about how different parts of systems – individuals, organizations and information – relate to one another. Consideration should be given not just to gathering information but also to understanding the significance of the information to different people. For example, a service user with mental health difficulties may inform you that they have stopped taking their medication and a close friend recently moved away. The practitioner may focus on the issue of medication whereas for the service user, this may pale into insignificance when compared with the issue of their friend moving away.

Following from this, we argue that a systems approach can help you to prioritize with regards to information. As mentioned previously, there is a danger that practitioners will experience 'information overload', having too much information and ending up feeling as if they cannot 'do' anything with it. According to Munro (2005), information overload is a real difficulty for practitioners and she argues that because service users inhabit complex systems, so do practitioners. This often results in practitioners trying to make sense of a wealth of information from lots of different sources, much of it frequently emotionally charged.

A systems approach offers one potential way out of this difficulty by enabling practitioners to habitually think about the information they are gathering. A systems approach suggests that information about the interactions between parts of the system is likely to more important and more significant than information simply about individuals. A clear example of this is that information related to how a parent and child interact is almost always more significant than simply gathering information about either the parent or the child on their own (see Wilkins 2010, 2011).

Practitioners may find the following list of questions useful as a guide when considering the information they have and the information they may need to obtain:

- Do all the pieces of information fit together? Do the pieces make sense to you?
- Are you sure about what the information means? Are there different ways of understanding the same information and if so, have you checked out what the actual meaning is?
- Can you verbally explain the situation to another person, such as a colleague, a manager or a service user? Verbalizing one's thoughts can help clarify the issues and highlight where the gaps are in your knowledge and understanding (see Chapter 9).
- Are you able to explain your emotions about the situation? Do you understand other people's emotional reactions and can you understand where they might be coming from?

Reflection point: information overload and 'analysis paralysis'

General Colin Powell, former Chairman of the Joint Chief of Staffs (1989–1993) and Secretary of State (2001–2005) in the United States of America, once gave a presentation on leadership. Powell argued that to be a good leader, he follows a formula of *P = (40 to*

70), in which *P* stands for the probability of success and the numbers 40–70 represent the percentage of information required. Powell argued that once the information was in the 40–70 range, he would 'go with his gut'.

By this, Powell is arguing that you do not need 100 per cent of the information in order to take action, instead, you need to consider the balance between taking action now, based on less than 100 per cent of the information you might ideally want, and waiting for more information to become available. Powell referred to the problem of 'analysis paralysis', noting that waiting to take action in the name of reducing risk can actually result in an increase in risk.

The question is, how much information is enough information?

In the extended case studies in Chapter 6, you might want to refer back to this reflection point and think about the amount of information you have, the total amount of information you might want and at what point it becomes more risky to wait than to take action now. Up to this point, we have been talking primarily about known information. However, a systems approach also encourages us to consider the practitioner as part of the system, rather than being above it or simply as a neutral element. Therefore, practitioners employing a basic systems approach will need to consider what impact they are having via their involvement. This is because a systems approach informs us that changing or intervening in one part of a system will have an impact on other parts as well and this could include unintended consequences. An example might be if you receive an anonymous referral from a neighbour regarding shouting, screaming and banging from the house next door. When you visit the family, you may tell them the referral is anonymous but they may either guess or suspect who told you – your visit could then lead to raised tensions between the two neighbours, creating further problems in future.

The implication of this, as we have argued before, is that assessment, analysis and help and support (intervention) should be seen as a dynamic and ongoing process and not something that has a neat and structured end point. Practitioners need to regularly reflect on their previous understandings and recommendations. A further implication of this approach is that practitioners should not see Referral, Assessment, Care Planning, and Review as distinct stages in a linear model, despite the design of many computer systems that social workers use.

Limitations of a basic systems approach

Arguably, an emphasis on systems – perhaps to the exclusion of individuals – is a drawback in practice, potentially leading to a loss of focus on the specific needs of a service user. Another potential difficulty is that by focusing on the 'intent' of systems to remain relatively static, this can lead to a failure to explain or explore change.

Therefore, notwithstanding recent discussions of systems approaches by Munro and the planned use of a systemic approach to future Serious Case Reviews, systemic approaches to practice are discussed less in the literature than has previously been the case, because of a lingering perception that such an approach cannot explain or account for change (Hudson 2000). According to Payne (2002), systemic thinking has been superseded by ecological thinking, which posits that a person's immediate environment has more bearing on their well being than more disparate systems.

Practice example: using a basic systems approach

A social worker in an Adults with Learning Disabilities team is asked to produce a 'transition plan' for Jackson, a disabled young adult, aged 20, who lives with his mother and sister in a four-bedroomed house. The referral was made by Jackson's sister, Debbie. The social worker visits Jackson's mother and is told that she is determined to be Jackson's carer and to keep him living at home. Debbie, a full-time nurse, tells you that she thinks Jackson needs to live more independently and she believes that with the right support, he will be able to. She also tells you that she and Jackson have an older brother. He has been in prison for the past year after being convicted of drink-driving. He is due to be released from prison soon and Jackson's mother has said he can move into the family home. Debbie also says that Jackson is very close to his older brother.

Using a systems approach, the social worker would want to consider (among other things) questions such as:

1   What are the systems involved in this case?
2   What are the individual reasons for keeping things the same (homeostatis) or change?

Potential answers might include:

1   *Jackson's older brother – a prison system, a 'criminal' system (we do not know enough about the drink-driving offence to say whether this is the case or not), a family system*

    Jackson – a family system

    Debbie – a work system, a family system

    Jackson's mother – a family system

    This indicates that although the referral is about Jackson, we actually appear to know more at this stage about Jackson's brother than about anyone else in the family.

2   *Jackson's older brother – may be likely to want things to 'stay the same' in terms of 'getting his old life back' or he may be looking to the future and hoping things will be very different. Does he have old relationships he wants to rekindle, for example? How might this impact on the family system?*

    Jackson – we do not know at this stage whether he wants to live at home or not. Clearly, this will be a very significant piece of information. A systems approach will also guide us to think about the significance of this piece of information. For example, what might it mean to his mother to find out, if she does not know already and if this is his view, that he does not want to live at home?

    Debbie – wants things to change but her reasons for this are not yet clear

    Jackson's mother – wants things to stay the same.

How do you think the above information would help guide your assessment of Jackson?

Ecological-transactional approach

The final and most complex model we have selected is an ecological-transactional approach. Because this approach is a development of an ecological approach, we will start by explaining the latter.

Ecological thinking arose out of the criticisms of systemic approaches discussed in the section above. Although the two approaches share some similarities – they both recognize the degree to which people exist within 'systems' – ecological thinking places more emphasis on immediate environmental interactions. This emphasis argues that the 'fit' between a person and their environment is actually the fit between their needs, goals and capacities to achieve them and the quality or nature of their physical and social environments. In simple terms, understanding only a person's needs or the risks they face and what they want to happen about them tells you very little. An ecological approach argues that you also need to obtain at least as good an understanding of the physical and social environment the person inhabits.

An example of this could be a disabled person with impaired mobility. This could result in the person needing a wheelchair, at times, to move around but knowing this *on its own* tells you very little about their day-to-day experiences. It is only by examining the 'fit' between this aspect of the person and their environment that you would be able to come to an understanding of how this actually affected them. You might find the fit to be highly favourable, because of the high prevalence of physical adaptations and a social acceptance of disabled people as full citizens with the same rights as anyone else. Or, you might find only an adequate fit or an unfavourable one. Thus, where a systemic approach might treat complex systems as essentially static, ecological thinking draws attention to the increased significance of local physical environments and the immediate impact of close family relations and the local society, treating these closer elements as more important.

As a development of ecological thinking, the ecological-transactional approach is also focused on individuals' interactions with their immediate environment. Such an approach sees the immediate environment as containing risk and protective factors. An individual's ability to 'withstand' the risk factors is understood as depending upon how protective factors are available to 'counter' them. Because the ecological-transactional approach is generally thought of as being related to human development, much of the literature in this area focuses on children. For example, Lynch and Cicchetti (1998) argued that children's ecological environments consist of the following levels:

- Ontogenic development, referring to the individual and their ability to develop and respond to their environment.
- Micro-system, referring to the child, their family and the environment of the child's everyday experiences. In other words, it is not individuals within the family that are thought to be significant so much as the dynamic they create

with the child. An example of this can be seen in a situation in which a child is living with two parents, one of whom is regularly violent towards the other. The issue of having a 'violent parent' is clearly of some significance but not as directly significant *for the child* as how the violence actually affects family life on a day-to-day basis.

- Exo-system, referring to the immediate (physical) environment around the home, including the local neighbourhood.
- Macro-system, referring to wider social issues such as the local culture and social beliefs which impact on the child and their family. An example would be a cultural pressure not to divorce, which may prevent a victimized parent from separating from a violent partner.

The ecological-transactional approach sees these four levels as nested within each other. A central idea of this approach is that our biological natures are in constant interaction with our environments and that these interactions produce outcomes together, which then impact on and interact with our development over time. Therefore, we can say that new development emerges from the interaction between a person's present and past experiences. Moreover, because the ecological-transactional approach informs us that every environment contains both risks and protective factors, new stages in development offer opportunities to 'correct' (or move away from) previous adverse outcomes, as well as presenting new potential risks. Accordingly, the ecological-transactional approach does not 'grade' developmental stages in terms of their importance but does recognize that 'developmental outcomes achieved early on . . . by virtue of being early, will interact with and influence later stages' (Brandon et al. 2008: 58). In other words, early experiences are important not because of any essential importance but simply because they happen before later experiences. Imagine setting off on a journey but with no fixed destination (like a road trip) and at the start of the journey, you flip a coin to decide whether you are going to head to the north or to the south. Although this decision is not in-and-of-itself any more or less important that later decisions to perhaps take the left or right turn in the road ahead, because it is an early decision it sets the overall pattern for the journey. So, the ecological-transactional approach encourages us to think about early experiences but not simply as a way of asking 'what happened in the past?' but 'how is what happened in the past seen as important in the present (and for the future)?'.

Limitations of an ecological-transactional approach

Although an ecological-transactional approach offers a robust framework for practice, it does appear to be more suitable for use in complex scenarios. There will clearly be areas of practice where such an approach is less useful. In other words, one of the reasons why an ecological-transactional approach is not always suitable is because of the principal of proportionality, that practitioners should intervene in private family life in as limited a way as possible to achieve the desired or required outcomes. As an ecological-transactional approach will always require asking detailed questions about family histories, it may not always be appropriate.

Applying an ecological-transactional approach in practice

When thinking about applying an ecological-transactional approach in practice, practitioners should certainly take note of the important idea that *cumulative risk factors* can have more of an impact than singular adverse events. Therefore, children or adults exposed to more risk factors over a longer period of time are likely to end up facing worse outcomes than children or adults exposed to fewer risk factors over a shorter period (MacKenzie et al. 2011). This partly explains the significance of neglect and the particularly poor outcomes that neglect can cause for children. In practice, this means that practitioners will often need to seek information beyond any 'presenting issues'. This is not always – or perhaps ever – easy to do. Social work departments are under pressure to make quick and clear decisions. This can lead to quite narrow assessments. For example, a referral may be received about a child being left at home alone. The response could be to consider whether the child was at risk for this period and if not, to close the case, without necessarily considering wider issues as to *why* the child was left alone and so on.

Practice example: using an ecological-transactional approach

A referral from a school informs you about a mother who collected her child from school with a blue bruise on their face. Keen to adhere to multi-disciplinary practice, you call the school for further information. There is limited additional information because the referred family have only recently moved to the locality. In the ensuing home visit, you find a tidy, warm and well organized home. The mother was welcoming and said that she had been told by the school of the referral. She explained that her bruise was caused when she fell off a chair while attempting to fit a curtain in their new home. The mother also revealed that her children were given money to buy their new beds by a charity near their previous home, where they moved to escape domestic violence from her previous partner who she divorced five years ago after 15 years of marriage.

On a superficial level, the information provided by the mother would in all likelihood justify the case being closed. However, contained within the example are two issues – poverty and previous domestic violence – that could warrant further exploration. In this example, an analytically minded practitioner may feel that 'case closure' is a premature decision and seek to explore these issues in more detail, for example, how the domestic violence impacted on the children, the stability of the family's income, the dynamic between the family's relative poverty and the previous violence and what the significance of this history is for current functioning.

However, as well as seeking the right information, the practitioner also needs to think about understanding the information in one of two ways, either *thematically* or *chronologically*. To analyse information thematically, a practitioner would need to recognize that everyone involved with a particular service user will have a different view, even if only slightly. A thematic analysis recognizes this explicitly and seeks to draw out key themes related to risk and protective factors shared by the different views.

A chronological analysis is not too dissimilar but involves mapping out *when* things have happened and searching for links between previous events and current functioning.

Practice example: using an ecological-transactional approach

Thinking about the above example, the practitioner may compile the following thematic analysis:

Key theme: poverty → moving to a new home (often expensive) → beds previously bought with help from a charity → explanation for the bruise involves putting up (new?) curtains

Key theme: domestic violence → divorced five years ago but only recently moved because of domestic violence → how did the domestic violence manifest itself over the five years (if it persisted for the duration)? → what prompted the move after five years (a build up of less significant events or one or two very significant events)?

How would a thematic analysis such as this help guide your assessment?

Task: Try to complete a chronological analysis based on the information we know at present. (N.B. This chronology will likely be quite short at this point but can still help identify where there are gaps in our knowledge.)

Risk and critical analysis

We hope that by now you will have started to think about how the three models discussed in this chapter are applicable in risk assessments. Given that assessing risk is now a significant or even central feature of many areas of social worker practice, this is clearly an important application. Having said this, it has been argued that assessing need and assessing risk are somewhat similar processes. As Kemshall has written, 'the identification of risk and the categorization of risks into thresholds for intervention and service delivery have become key mechanisms in the rationing of scarce social care resources' (2002: 82). In other words, assessing risk is one way that practitioners may be asked to assist with decisions about the use of resources to meet needs.

When thinking about risk, it can be helpful to look to sociological literature on risk (Warner and Sharland 2010). Although this is a broad field, we want to simplify the discussion and suggest that broadly, there are two approaches to risk: the 'risk society' approach considers risk to be a *real thing* in society while 'social construction' approaches consider risk to be a dynamic creation (i.e. it is not really there until it is 'noticed', usually by professionals working for statutory agencies). Much of this work is complex and goes beyond the scope of this particular book but essentially, the latter approach views risk as being 'constructed' rather than inherent. Risks identified by social workers arise from human interactions and broader socio-economic inequalities and as such, risks are not inherent within service users or their families but rather, professionals interpret certain situations as risky through their assessments. In other words, risks do not really exist until social workers or other professionals identify them and describe them.

On the other hand, the risk society approach argues that risks arise as unavoidable consequences of social relations; therefore, they exist irrespective of whether we can identify them or not. From this perspective, the social worker's role is to identify, categorize and describe the risks which exist in service users' lives – and then to help reduce those risks (see Mäntysaari 2005, for a fuller discussion). We will consider these different views of risk in more detail in the next section.

Real or constructed?

Risk society ideas in social work consider risks to be hazards that we face in our everyday lives, irrespective of the activities we are engaged in. Here the question of risk is based on the probability of an undesired outcome occurring. As such, and as you will no doubt find in practice, assessing the possibility of risk occurring in the future will necessarily involve balancing the possible harms that may occur with the likelihood of those harmful events actually happening. As Webb argues, 'the recognition and assessment of the uncertainty (of risk) provides the basis for understanding the relation between judgement and uncertainty' (Webb 2006: 34).

Although the idea of risks as outlined above may seem somewhat obvious to modern sensibilities, this has not always been the case. According to Beck (1992), in the past risks were seen as 'natural' and to some degree, unavoidable. The reaction of much of the popular press to examples of when children have been killed (e.g. Peter Connolly) would seem to confirm that it is no longer acceptable to simply say a risk was unavoidable – the question is often posed of what might have been done to prevent it. The fast pace of modern life has also caused changes in the 'traditional' pillars of society – class, ethnicity, family, nation, settled employment – which used to mitigate the downside of progress by making us feel more secure. Consequently, we are more sensitive to unpredictability and because of the mass media, we are more quickly made aware of disasters in other parts of the world, which further increases our perceptions that the world is more risky. Put together, these issues appear to put governments under pressure to 'do something' and they have typically responded by increasing regulations.

From the viewpoint of statutory services, and as Kemshall et al. (1997) have argued, reduced public spending inevitably results in much tighter eligibility or threshold criteria. This had led to a concentration on people deemed to be most 'in need', which often means those perceived to be most 'at risk' (or those who are perceived as posing the most risk). Therefore, at the same time as feelings of insecurity have increased, there are fewer resources to deal with those insecurities.

Constructionist perspectives see risk in a different way, and view risk as being created by human interpretation and not necessarily arising as the outcome of human relations. Risks are only identified when professionals choose to classify particular aspects of people's behaviour or relations as risky. This has led some to argue that child protection policies are instruments for intervening in families to shape children's development according to targets set by the government (Parton 1998). Parton also argues that these policies rely on amassing a lot of data on children and in the process, it can be difficult to notice or understand the reality of the child's day-to-day experiences (Parton 2008). This is something that particularly concerned Professor Munro in her recent review of child protection in England (Munro 2011b).

In attempting to draw helpful links between this sociological literature on risk and social work practice 'on the ground', we will start by saying that in our experience, practitioners do tend to understand that child protection systems and other social work systems of protection do have certain features of risk being constructed by professionals. This can be seen in the differences between practitioners about what risks a service user may be exposed to and the significance of these risks. This suggests to us that risk is not a real phenomenon which can be easily measured. Rather, it is a question of looking at individual circumstances and making a judgement about the risk to the individual. Again, this is something Professor Munro is very keen for child protection social workers to do, to exercise more professional judgement rather than following centrally prescribed policies and procedures.

This can be a more difficult judgement to make with adults than children, simply because children are – surely correctly – considered to be more vulnerable than adults and therefore, thresholds for statutory intervention are necessarily lower. With adults, there is often a difficult judgement to be made not only about the level of risk but about the adult's capacity to understand that risk. Because adults are considered to have the mental capacity to make decisions, and in most cases keep themselves safe, social workers have no duty to intervene in their lives (unless children are involved). Recently, the Mental Capacity Act 2005 (MCA) introduced the important concept of 'unwise' decision-making (Department for Constitutional Affairs 2005). As prescribed by the MCA, every adult has the right to lead their lives as they wish even if they engage in activities that professionals deem risky or 'unwise'. The unwise decision principle again highlights the constructionist approach to risk that practitioners are asked to take – it is not the activity or decision itself that is inherently risky but the risk of any 'unwise decision' must be negotiated between the adult in question and the relevant professional network.

The final application to social work practice is in the role of formal and informal reasoning in critical analysis (as discussed in Chapters 1 and 2). We wish again to highlight the importance of understanding these different ways of thinking and the interplay between them. These two ways or systems of thinking direct us to different kinds of information and especially where risk is concerned, the informal system is likely to be particularly involved (think back to the example of Spock walking in the forest and the reaction of the informal system to a perceived risk from a snake; see p. 48).

As we have seen from the constructionist approach to risk, identifying and assessing risk cannot simply be a matter of collecting facts. We must also allow for the critical analysis of those facts. At a personal level, as social workers we have our own emotional reactions to risk that cannot be separated from our professional assessments. All these issues make risk assessments such a challenge to social work: we are asked to focus on objective factors but at the same time, avoiding the subjective is not possible.

We conclude this section by saying that the advanced analytically-minded social worker will benefit from acknowledging that risk assessment is both realist and social constructionist. There are certain 'hard' facts that we need in order to make decisions about risk; however, the most effective judgements will surely recognize that certain events or groups usually first provoke emotions in us or others before the risk assessments formally begins.

Summary and conclusions

In this chapter we have discussed three approaches to critical analysis. We have suggested that SWOT is useful because it is relatively easy to apply in practice through the application of four quadrants by which social workers can visually present case information. However, it is not always possible to distinguish between advantages and disadvantages of various interventions. As postulated by basic systems theory, an intervention which one person resonates through their social network, therefore it is important for practitioners to take a holistic view – for example how the person and their interaction with immediate and wider networks will be affected by practitioners' actions. In this sense the basic systems approach is useful in drawing attention to the fact that people and their families exist within wider social networks. Taking these ideas further, an ecological-transactional approach is applicable in more complex cases. This approach helps draw attention to how accumulated inequality and trauma impact on people's decision-making in later life (including their style of parenting). Finally we have discussed realist and constructionist approaches to risk, and argued that more effective interventions are likely to be those that integrate both approaches. Altogether these models discussed in this chapter portray a different kind of practice: one of relationship-based therapeutic practice (Ruch 2005) through which practitioners work in conjunction with families to identify their challenges and strengths. The models presented in this chapter also highlight the importance of values in social work practice. Both service users and professionals have values, which shape their actions: a transparent discussion of values therefore helps both parties understand their motivations, and in the case of service users, the desire to change.

Key points from this chapter include

- SWOT, basic systems theory, ecological-transactional model and risk analysis can be applied in cases of differing complexity.
- Ecological-transactional model and risk analysis should be applied in complex cases such as child protection where it is important to understand parental family history and motivation to change.
- The three models discussed in this chapter offer another means to understand service users and their families; however, social workers have to exercise some judgements in their application to practice.
- The models draw attention to a relationship-based approach to practice: practitioners should draw on empathy, understanding, respect for other people's values and social work skills of communication to enable service users to overcome life's challenges.

Recommended reading

Brandon, M., Belderson, P., Warren, C. et al. (2008) *Analysing Child Deaths and Serious Injury Through Abuse and Neglect: What Can we Learn?* Department of Children, Schools and Families. https://www.education.gov.uk/publications/eOrderingDownload/DCSF-RR023.pdf (accessed 30 May 2012).

Ruch, G., Turney, D. and Ward, A. (2010) *Relationship-based Social Work: Getting to the Heart of Practice.* London: Jessica Kingsley Press.

Wulczyn, F., Daro, D., Fluke, J. et al. (2010) *Adapting a Systems Approach to Child Protection: Key Concepts and Considerations.* http://www.unicef.org/spanish/protection/files/Adapting_Systems_Child_Protection_Jan_2010.pdf (accessed 9 May 2012).

Kemshall, H. (2010) Risk rationalities in contemporary social work policy and practice, *British Journal of Social Work*, 40(4): 1247–62.

5 Tools for critical analysis

Chapter overview

By the end of this chapter, you should have an understanding of:

- A range of tools that can help with critical analysis and what they are
- How to use the various tools we present in practical situations
- How the use of these tools contributes to building an analytical mindset

Introduction

In this chapter, we are going to look at three specific tools for developing and refining your analytical mindset. Much like in the previous chapter, where we considered four models or approaches for analytical practice, we do not intend that you will apply these tools exactly as they are laid out here. This is especially important when you consider that in Chapter 1, we argued that critical analysis is not best thought of as a separate stage in a formal assessment but as a more general approach to thinking and to practice in general. Our intention is that these tools will be useful for you as a way of practising to think more analytically. You may well take forward some of the ideas underpinning these tools or even elements of them into your practice – indeed, there is good evidence that using these tools as they are set out here can make practitioners feel more confident about their decision-making (Dalzell and Sawyer 2011). Nevertheless, we would not be overly concerned if readers became familiar with the tools and then moved on to practise in a less formulaic way. Because of this, you should not be too concerned if you feel, having read about and practised these tools, that it is unrealistic for you to translate them into your day-to-day work.

Therefore, for each tool, we will set out what the tool is and how it is useful. We will then demonstrate the use of each tool with some practical examples and we will set some exercises for you to complete in order to become more familiar with each one.

The tools

We have selected four tools for you to use and explore and we have selected these four tools in particular because we believe they will help you practise different facets of critical, analytical thinking.

Cultural review

The first tool we have selected is a cultural review. A cultural review is a way of examining one's own cultural assumptions about a service user and their situation. This tool can be seen in the light of Chapter 1 and the discussion about values and beliefs and the effect these can have on our interpretation of apparently objective facts. The idea of a cultural review can be linked back to the work of McCracken (1988), who wrote about the importance of cultural principles and how they help individuals to make sense of the world. Although McCracken was writing about consumer goods, the idea that culture is a lens through which people coordinate 'social action and productive activity, specifying the behaviours and objects that issue from both' (1988: 73) is applicable in a much wider sense. McCracken also noted that this process is bi-directional; in other words, an individual's actions can contribute to a process of revising cultural values. Luna and Gupta (2001) give the example of how an initiation ritual into gang membership can alter or reinforce the individual's cultural values, thus cementing them into the group (p. 51).

The importance of understanding a service user's culture is evident from such cases as 'Baby Diamond'. Baby Diamond died in Waltham Forest in 2010; her death was a result of force-feeding by her mother, who was originally from Ghana. In some parts of Ghana, the force-feeding of an underweight child is viewed as culturally acceptable (*Guardian* 2011). Unfortunately, the concern of the social workers in this case focused on the risk of using excessive force to feed the baby, rather than on the risk of harm from the act of force-feeding itself (Community Care 2011). Turney et al. (2011) have noted the potential for mistakes being made because of 'cultural misunderstandings', such as seems to have happened in the case of Baby Diamond.

Burton (2009) recommends the use of a cultural review at the outset of work with service users in order to alert us to any 'assumptions, prejudices or simple lack of knowledge [that] may have a bearing on [our] response to the family and the approach taken to working with them' (p. 8).

So, what is a cultural review? It is a method for considering what assumptions you might be making about a service user based on 'cultural categories', such as beliefs, gender, disability status and social status. The aim of a cultural review is to alert you to any areas in which your own assumptions or lack of knowledge may impact on your practice. When completing a cultural review, it is important to be as honest about your own views and prejudices as possible. Without a significant level of honesty, a cultural review is not very useful. It's probably easier at this point to show you an example.

Practice example: cultural review tool

A cultural review involves answering the following questions with regards to a particular service user (see Dalzell and Sawyer 2011):

1   What do I know about the individuals and families with this particular cultural background or life experience?
2   Where does my knowledge come from?
3   What prejudices may I hold (positive or negative)?
4   What do I know/expect about people of this (these) age(s), their lives and needs?
5   What might surprise me about this family and why would it be a surprise?
6   How might this family/the parents/child/siblings/community perceive me?
7   How might my assessment and my agency be perceived?
8   What impact might the assessment have on the family's lives and on their perception of their lives?
9   What agency norms and practices do I take with me on an assessment (for example, awareness of risk thresholds, of 'good enough' parenting, resource restrictions)?

Using the example of Daisy, who we first introduced in Chapter 1 (pp. 13–14), we might complete a cultural review as follows:

1   I grew up in a poor, working-class area and because of these experiences, I believe I have a personal insight with this family that other workers do not have. I know families like this one (and mine) can be proud and defensive against what they see as outside interference; drinking is part of the culture but most people like this drink quite heavily and still manage.
2   Practice experience; the media; my own background.
3   That stepfathers are more often a negative than a positive impact for children; mothers who allow men with criminal records to have contact with their children are placing their own needs above those of their children's; domestic violence is highly likely in this situation; Daisy's mother is largely or wholly responsible for her care; that mother's partner takes more money out of the family than he puts in; that mother's partner is only interested in Daisy's mother and not in Daisy (i.e. he feels no particular bond with Daisy).
4   I would expect Daisy's mother to prioritize Daisy's needs over her own; I would expect a male of this age to be working and bringing money into the family home; I would expect Daisy to have her own bedroom.
5   If mother's partner had a significant role in caring for Daisy it would surprise me because of my assumption that for people of this background, child care is primarily a female responsibility; if Daisy's biological father had any significant role in her life it would surprise me because my practice experience is largely of absent rather than involved fathers; if mother's partner were more of a protective factor for Daisy than a risk factor it would surprise me because men, especially men unrelated to children, are usually talked of in terms of the negative impacts they can have rather than the positives; if Daisy had a secure attachment to her mother or her mother's partner it

would surprise me because this would suggest that largely, Daisy was in a predictable and responsive caregiving environment.

6   As an authority figure; as an intruder; as someone who wants to tell them how to parent; as someone who could help get some money for them.

7   My assessment might be seen as a waste of time, an intrusive process; my agency might be seen as a powerful entity, able to remove children if parents do not conform with our expectations.

8   The assessment could cause stress to the family, it could highlight some difficulties (e.g. mother's problem drinking) that otherwise are not really talked about. It could make things difficulty between the nursery and the family, given that the nursery made the referral to social care – it could even lead to Daisy being withdrawn from the nursery.

9   Thresholds – does this meet my team's criteria for involvement? Is there anyone else I could refer this on to? My team does not really do 'child in need' support – if this is not child protection, I will have to close the case. How can I persuade my manager that this is 'child protection', so I can keep the case open?

The value of using this tool is in alerting practitioners to the narratives they have constructed around a particular culture, family or service user. It can also ensure we are focusing on answering the right questions. For example, in the case of Baby Diamond, one possible explanation for what happened is that practitioners may have been seeking to answer the question of whether excessive force was being used to feed the child rather than asking why the child was being force fed and what the risks are of force feeding, even when excessive force is not being used.

Needs analysis

The second tool we have selected is a needs analysis. In any area of social work, there can often be a tension between assessing risk versus need. Where practitioners are focused exclusively on risk, this tends to lead to a focus on family and individual dysfunction rather than anything else (Seden 2001). A focus on risk over need has led to the development of various tools in order to improve the accuracy of decisions, including through the use of computerized risk assessment models. In practice, these models have not proven to be all that useful for practitioners (Munro 2002) and Dalzell and Sawyer (2011) argue for a more balanced approach between assessing need and risk. This strikes us as a good thing to aim for but as Cleaver and Walker (2004) have shown, many practitioners struggle to assess and analyse needs.

In our experience, practitioners can seem to range between over-complicating assessments of needs and over-generalizing them. For example, when considering the family and social relationships of a child with learning disabilities, we have seen many examples of assessments that conclude that the child's needs in this area are being met because they live at home with their birth family. This is too general. Equally, we have seen many examples of assessments that argue the child needs to attend specific and particular cultural groups, perhaps related to their parents' religion or ancestral country of origin. This is often an over-complication. There is also a well-known tendency to think about services before being clear about needs and outcomes. As we argued in Chapter 1, being clear about outcomes can make the process of helping and supporting a service user a good deal easier.

For example, if a child is assessed as needing to develop their social relationships with peers (to make and keep friends), the temptation can be to identify the service (such as an after school group) before thinking about the outcome – in other words, are we looking for the child to be able to talk about two close friends, for the child to be seen to play regularly with other children of a similar age or for the child to be invited to a birthday party at a friend's house? All of these could be said to be meeting the child's need for social relationships with peers. What we need to be clear about, though, is what specifically are we looking to happen, in order to know that the need for this child to develop social relationships has been met? Simply going to an after school group will not be enough if the child remains, for example, withdrawn or ostracized by peers and so on.

The National Children's Bureau (Williams and McCann 2006) has produced a framework to help practitioners think about the needs of service users more clearly and it is their framework that we will demonstrate here (see Table 5.1). The framework is a very simple one, listing domains of need, relating these to the service user and the outcomes being sought. Although the framework has been designed for children – and we use an 8-year-old child named John in our example – the framework is simple enough that it can easily be adapted for use with adults as well. In our example, we have included two responses for each row – the top example in each row is meant to be an example of a 'too general' response with the lower example being more specific and hence more useful. The aim of the framework is to prompt practitioners to think more clearly about outcomes and to link these to specific needs. You may have noticed already that the framework does not include services. This is deliberate, for the reasons cited above; namely, the tendency to identify service before being clear what outcomes you are aiming for.

Decision trees

The final tool we have selected is a decision tree. As discussed in Chapter 1, critical analysis and decision-making are distinct activities; nevertheless, the *ultimate aim* of critical analysis is to inform better decision-making. Therefore, we tend to view the decision tree not as a way of helping practitioners to make real or actual decisions in their work – although it can be used in this way – but more as an aid to clear thinking. We believe the tool can help you do this by prompting, again, a focus on outcomes but also to spend some time thinking about the likelihood of each reasonably available outcome actually happening. As a result, it can help you think about what might need to be done to increase the likelihood of desirable outcomes and reduce the likelihood of less desirable ones. The tool can also highlight where any gaps might exist in your knowledge.

As with the two tools already discussed, decision trees are relatively simply. To start using a decision tree, you first need to identify what the potential outcomes are for the

Table 5.1 Needs analysis

	Needs	Outcomes
Health	John needs to be healthy	For John to be healthy
	John needs to keep his teeth clean and healthy	For John to brush his teeth twice a day
Education	John needs to be in school	For John to attend school
	John has poor school attendance and needs to be in school sufficiently for him to keep up with the curriculum	For John to achieve 90 per cent attendance between now and the next school holiday
Emotional and behavioural development	John needs to build his self-esteem	For John to feel good about himself
	John has said he is being bullied at school and this makes him feel bad about himself	For John to feel safe at school – school staff to investigate any bullying and stop it
Identity	John needs to have his own identity	For John to understand who he is and his culture
	John needs to develop his own sense of identity by doing things apart from the rest of his family that give him confidence and which he enjoys	For John to be asked which activities or things he knows he is good at – for John to be given at least one chance a week to do something he is good at
Family and social relationships	John needs positive relationships	For John to get on with his parents and with friends
	John needs to develop friendships with other children	For John to be able to name two friends at school and for John to have a birthday party at home and invite his friends to play
Social presentation	John needs to present well	For John to present well
	For John to have some control over what he wears when he goes out	For John to go shopping with his mother or father and buy some clothes that he chooses, with guidance from his parents
Self-care skills	John needs to learn to take care of himself	John to develop age appropriate self-care skills
	John needs to learn to brush his teeth on his own	For John to go shopping with his mother or father, buy a new toothbrush and toothpaste and be shown how to brush his teeth twice a day

service user – ideally, you would do this in partnership with the service user rather than simply on your own. You need to think about the potential benefit of each outcome and the likelihood of achieving each one. You need to do this numerically and we will show you what we mean in the example below. By multiplying together the potential benefit with the likelihood of success, you achieve an overall 'rating' number for each outcome. The figures for the potential benefit and the likelihood of success are input by whoever is using the tool. It is important to remember that these figures are subjective and hence the decision remains a judgement call – a decision tree is not a mechanistic device to remove decision-making power from real people. It is probably best thought of more as a guide for you and the service user. The best way to illustrate this is with an example.

Practice example: decision tree – a service user in hospital

You are working with a service user with mental health difficulties who is currently an in-patient at hospital. Medical staff inform you that the service user is now ready for discharge and you need to develop a support plan. Based on what you know of the service user, including their wishes and feelings, you conclude that there are three possible options to choose from. The service user could return to their own home with community support services, they could reside with a family member for a period of time or they could move into 'sheltered accommodation'. You decide to complete a decision tree to help you and the service user think about each option in more detail.

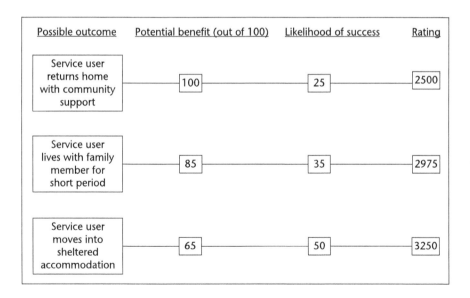

Possible outcome	Potential benefit (out of 100)	Likelihood of success	Rating
Service user returns home with community support	100	25	2500
Service user lives with family member for short period	85	35	2975
Service user moves into sheltered accommodation	65	50	3250

You conclude from the decision tree that the outcome of a return home with community support is the most beneficial option but also the least likely to succeed. The least preferred option – that of sheltered accommodation – is also the most likely to succeed with the middle option of living with family being somewhere in the middle for both potential benefit and likelihood of success. Overall, this would suggest that the 'best' course of action is to arrange sheltered accommodation for the service user. However, it is important to remember that the decision tree is not a method of dictating to you and the service user what should happen. One way of using this tool could be to look at what might be needed in order to increase the likelihood of success for the preferred option of returning home or to increase the potential benefit of a short-term placement with family members. In order to illustrate this further, we are including another example.

Practice example: decision tree – working with a disabled child

You are working with a disabled child who is having difficulty accessing mainstream social activities and groups. Her parents have asked for your help in ensuring their child can socialize and they can have regular breaks.

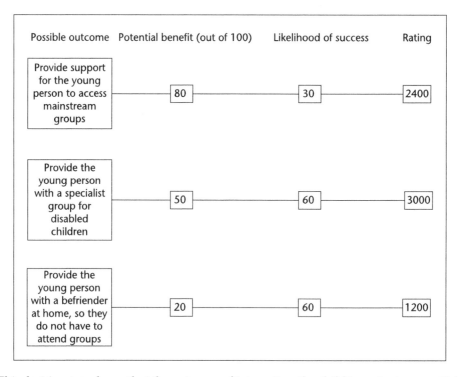

This decision tree shows that the outcome of integrating the child in mainstream activities has the highest potential benefit but the lowest likelihood of success. The other two options are seen as being equal in terms of how likely they are to succeed but providing the child with an individual befriender has a low potential benefit, meaning that the highest rating is for the provision of specialist groups. Again, this does not dictate what should be done. It may be that the child or her parents have strong views about using mainstream activities and as with the previous example, you may use this decision tree as a prompt to explore *why* the likelihood of success of mainstream groups appears to be so much lower than the other two potential outcomes. If support and help could be put in place to increase the likelihood of success of mainstream groups by just 10 points, perhaps by providing the staff with some basic disability awareness training, the overall rating for this option would increase to 3200, making it the highest rated option overall.

One way in which this tool can prompt better critical analysis is by encouraging practitioners to justify why they have chosen certain numbers for certain columns and rows. For example, why is it felt that the likelihood of success for the mainstream groups is half that for the specialist groups or a befriender? Putting yourself in a position to have to explain these numbers to a colleague, manager or service user will likely ensure that your analysis is as critical and robust as possible and reduce the prevalence of more 'woolly' thinking.

Reflection point

Thinking about service users and potential outcomes in terms of numbers in a decision tree can often feel uncomfortable for social workers. It can feel reductionist – that is, it reduces complex situations and people into a single number (the 'rating'). However, we would invite you to reflect on how you currently make decisions. As long as you consider at least two different possible outcomes when making decisions with service users, you must already be engaging in some form of balancing or weighing-up between them. If so, how would you explain to someone else how you go about this process of balancing or weighing-up? Would you be able to explain it as clearly as in a decision tree? If not, what might be the potential ethical issues or difficulties with the balancing or weighing-up process being essentially 'hidden inside your head'?

Practice example

In this section, we are going to provide a relatively extensive practice example for you to consider. The aim of this exercise is to apply each of the three tools we have outlined above to the example.

Exercise 11 Applying tools for critical analysis

This exercise is a continuation of Exercise 9 (Chapter 2), in which we introduced Mrs Bee. It may be helpful to turn to Exercise 9 now (pp. 43–4), if you have not already completed it.

Briefly, in Exercise 9, you (the social worker) had completed a home visit to see Mrs Bee and her daughter Joan. Joan was convinced that Mrs Bee is not safe to live on her own and felt she may need residential care. Mrs Bee felt equally as strongly this was not the case. During your visit, you noticed that Mrs Bee was slightly repetitive in the stories she told you and that she was somewhat vague about some of the details.

From that first visit, you also learn that Mrs Bee is a black female, aged 73. She describes herself as a Christian but said she does not go to Church. Peter, the eldest child, is 49, Joan is 46 and Matthew is 45. Mr Bee, father of Peter and Joan, died four years ago. Mr Johnson, father of

Matthew, is a white male, aged 69. Mr Johnson and Mrs Bee are separated and Mr Johnson has no contact with any of the family – Mrs Bee and Matthew are not sure where he lives. Mrs Bee says she enjoys watching horse racing and that when she was younger, she used to work at a racecourse for a firm of bookies. Mrs Bee says she grew up in the Caribbean but moved to Manchester when she was in her early 30s. She met Mr Bee in Manchester; he also grew up in the Caribbean. They married and remained married until Mr Bee's death. Mrs Bee and Mr Johnson met through Mrs Bee's work and they had a brief extra-marital relationship, which ended when Mrs Bee became pregnant with Matthew.

Task 1

Based on what you know so far, complete a cultural review of the family.

You might then find it useful to answer the following questions:

1   What assumptions have you made about this family? How might you check out those assumptions in practice (what steps would you take to do so)?
2   Would your practice look any different if Mrs Bee and family were white and middle class? If yes, how and why? If not, why not?

The day after your initial visit, you receive a telephone call from Peter, Mrs Bee's eldest child. He is direct with you, saying that Mrs Bee does not need residential care and he will not allow it. He describes Joan as well meaning but feels she spends too much time with Mrs Bee and is becoming obsessive. He says he feels Joan needs a job as this will broaden her horizons but alludes to difficulties which prevent her from obtaining employment. You ask what he means and he becomes vague, saying Joan can be overprotective. He refuses to discuss what would happen to Mrs Bee's home if she did leave. You suggest a family group meeting, to which everyone agrees.

Mrs Bee, Peter, Joan and a third sibling, Matthew, attend the meeting. Peter appears to be 'siding' with Mrs Bee over the issue of residential care. Joan says she remains concerned and tells you that only yesterday, Mrs Bee got lost and the police were called to bring her home. Mrs Bee says she was just visiting a friend and points out she was unharmed. Mrs Bee questions the need for the meeting and appears to be getting agitated. Matthew seems to defer to Peter's views.

The day after the meeting, Joan contacts you to say that the police have brought Mrs Bee home again, at around 9 p.m., after she was found 'wandering' in a nearby street. Mrs Bee is unharmed but Joan expresses frustration that no one seems to understand how vulnerable her mother is. Joan begs you to arrange a residential placement. Joan has contacted Mrs Bee's GP, who has referred her for a mental health assessment. Joan reports that the GP is also of the view that a residential placement is required. You contact the GP who confirms this is her view and reports that Joan often contacts her, distressed about her mother's behaviour.

A few weeks later, you receive a report from a consultant psychiatrist saying that Mrs Bee is 'pleasantly confused – an engaging lady with some cognitive impairments'. However, the report indicates that her condition is not acute. You decide to call another family group meeting.

The second family group meeting is notably more heated that the first. Joan is now even more convinced that a residential placement is required, citing the GP's recommendation. Peter remains equally as convinced that there is nothing particularly wrong with Mrs Bee, saying her memory has deteriorated to some degree but this is a result of her age. Peter cites the report of the consultant psychiatrist in support of his view. He says a residential placement would be a violation of his mother's human rights. Matthew suggests Mrs Bee stay at home but with some form of technology to support her, such as a tracking device so she could be easily found if she went out on her own.

Task 2

Based on what you know so far, complete a decision tree for Mrs Bee.

As you do so, ask yourself the following questions:

1   How have I decided what the options are that should be included in the decision tree? What options have I excluded and what is my basis for excluding them?
2   On what basis have I selected the numbers to insert in the 'potential benefit' and 'likeli- hood' columns? What might persuade me to change the numbers? Have I massaged the figures to suit my preferred figures? How could I defend against the possibility that I have?
3   How might a decision tree completed by Mrs Bee, Peter or Joan look like? What is the significance of any differences that might exist between their decision trees and mine?

The day after the second family group meeting, you receive a call from the police. Mrs Bee has been found walking on the motorway and has been taken to hospital, where she has now been sectioned under the Mental Health Act because she is presenting as a danger to herself. You visit Mrs Bee in hospital and she remembers who you are and thanks you for your kind visit. She recalls the incident reported to you by the police but is inaccurate in many of the details. However, she is aware she is in hospital and reports that the nurses are 'quite nice really'. She tells you she is looking forward to going home and asks how soon this will be.

Task 3

Based on what you know so far, complete a needs analysis of Mrs Bee.

As you do so, ask yourself the following questions:

1   How does the needs analysis help with your decision-making about Mrs Bee?
2   Does the needs analysis and clear identification of the outcomes change the decision tree you completed previously? If so, how? If not, why not?

You can see an example of how we completed this exercise in Appendix 8.

Summary and conclusions

In this chapter, we have set out three tools that you can use to help develop your analytical mindset. As we have shown with the practice examples, these tools can certainly be applicable to individual work with service users and there is no harm and likely much benefit in doing so. As we have stressed throughout the book, analysis happens best when it involves more than one person – i.e. more than just you, working on your own – and one particular benefit of these tools is that they can quite easily be used with a colleague, with your manager in supervision but also directly with service users. Using, say, a decision tree directly with a service user can make your practice more transparent (because you will be setting out explicitly what outcomes are available based on factors such as your agency's norms and resources) but also more equal because there may be outcomes that seem preferable to you but which the service user may strongly object to.

However, although these tools can be used in this way, our view is that most practitioners will feel they do not have the time to use these tools directly in practice. Student practitioners may feel they do have the time and, as we say above, there is much benefit in this. If you feel you do not have the time, then the benefit for you may be to practise with these tools, both by using the practice examples contained in the book but also perhaps with a number of your service users. In this way, you will become accustomed to thinking more analytically and this practice will then be likely to extend to your other case work, even if you are not using the tools directly with every service user.

Key points from this chapter include

- Summarizing information is a key part of analysis but analysis is more than providing a good summary.
- Critical analysis is not a separate 'event' – an analytical mindset or approach needs to pervade everything you do as a social worker.
- Without good analysis, it is unlikely you will be able to make sound judgements and the best available decisions.

Recommended reading

Dalzell, R. and Sawyer, E. (2011) *Putting Analysis into Assessment: Undertaking Assessments of Need – A Toolkit for Practitioners*, 2nd revised edition. London: NCB.

6 Guided case examples

Chapter overview

By the end of this chapter, you should understand how to apply the tools, approaches and thinking of the preceding chapters to the two extended case examples.

How to use these case examples

The aim of this chapter, and of the two extended case examples we have selected, is to allow you to put into practice the ideas, tools and models we have discussed earlier in the book. Unlike with the practice examples in the previous chapters, in this chapter we will limit the number of prompts we provide, in order that you have an opportunity to engage in some critical analytical thinking without worrying what we might think about the same example. You might feel that you want to go back to certain chapters, to refresh your memory of particular tools or methods, and we have provided page references to help with this. You may also find it helpful to look again (or for the first time!) at the Appendices, where we have included several examples of how we have completed the practice exercises in the book so far. The overall aim is for you to analyse the case examples and to answer questions such as 'why are things happening?'. Although we have made some suggestions as to which tools or approaches you might want to use at particular points, please note that these are not meant to be prescriptive – part of developing your analytical mindset is knowing when and how to use particular approaches and therefore we do not intend to 'spoon feed' you the 'answers' or prompt you too much about how to get them. You may find this hard work and as we saw in the Introduction, hard thinking is like hard physical work – sometimes, people prefer to simply avoid it. We would simply say, do not give up!

We have selected both of these examples from situations that we have both been involved in so we are confident that they will have a ring of authenticity to them and hopefully you will see parallels with service users or situations that you may also have experienced. All names and some other details have been changed to protect the anonymity and confidentiality of all concerned.

Case examples overview

We have selected the two examples to cover four areas of practice – disabled children, child protection, adult mental health and older adults. As is common in real life practice, there are many elements of crossover in the two case examples – for example, in the first, you will be asked to think about working with a disabled child about whom you were concerned and a mother with mental health difficulties, hence combining three areas of practice in one example. For both examples, we have followed the same layout. We begin by providing a genogram of the service user and their family. We will then go through the case example stage by stage – each stage will include a brief chronology and a summary of the situation. You will then be prompted to analyse what you know so far and think about what you might do next. Remember, the point of analysis is ultimately to enable better decision-making but in these examples, we would encourage you to focus less on clear decision-making and more on thinking about the 'whys' and the 'hows' of the situation. As outlined above, how you approach the critical analysis is left up to you. This is your chance to practise and develop your analytical mindset and much like learning a foreign language, practice makes perfect. You should of course feel free to refer back to previous chapters of the book for reminders of particular tools, models or approaches that you might find useful.

Case example 1 – children

In this case example, you are the social worker for Abigail Bello, a young woman with learning difficulties and severe scoliosis (curvature of the spine, affecting Abigail's mobility and posture). At the outset of the case example, Abigail is 12 years old.

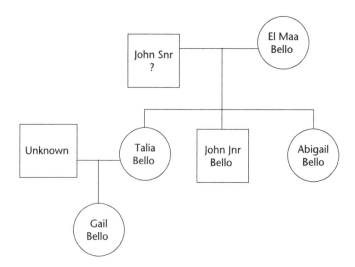

Figure 6.1 Genogram

Part 1

Table 6.1 Chronology

Date	Event
25/01/2008	Ms Bello contacted out-of-hours team to say she and her children would soon be dead
26/01/2008	Referral from Drug and Alcohol support service – Ms Bello needs support from social services
27/01/2008	Referral from Occupational Therapy – Abigail has a deformed spine and needs assistance with personal care
04/02/2008	Initial Assessment completed

You complete your Initial Assessment and conclude that Abigail is a 'child in need' (s17, Children Act 1989) because she is disabled. Abigail has difficulty with personal care especially in the mornings when she likes to take a bath or shower. Abigail also has difficulty attending mainstream activities as she finds it difficult to make friends and feels 'out of her depth' in such settings.

During your first home visit, El Maa informs you that she considers herself to be a very spiritual person but without belonging to any particular faith. At various times, El Maa has considered herself to be a Muslim, a Jehovah's Witness and a Pagan. El Maa considers her black heritage to be a crucial part of her identity and regularly attends cultural events such as black film festivals and museum exhibitions during national events such as Black History Month. El Maa reports having a troubled childhood. Her maternal aunt raised her as her birth mother felt unable to care for her and left when she was around 3 months of age. El Maa does not know who her father is. During the visit, Abigail appears to be well presented, clean and happy. El Maa informs you that she has no intention of harming herself or her children and that she only said this when she was in a very 'bad place'.

You also gather the following information – El Maa Bello is a black British female, aged 38. John Snr, about whom very little is known, is a black British male, aged 54. John Snr is the father of Abigail and John Jnr; Talia has a different father about whom nothing is known. John Jnr is 15 and Talia is 17. John Jnr lives at home with El Maa and Talia is accommodated in foster care. Talia was accommodated when she was 4 years old as El Maa felt unable to cope – Talia has remained in care ever since.

You also contact the Drug and Alcohol support service and El Maa's key worker informs you that El Maa has a personality disorder and a history of substance misuse and relapse.

Reflection and analysis point

At this point in the case example, reflect back on what you know so far about Abigail and her family. You might want to consider completing one or both of the following:

- modified SWOT analysis (see p. 56)
- a basic systems analysis (see p. 59)

You might also want to consider completing a cultural review (see p. 74) and a needs analysis (see p. 76).

Once you have completed the above tasks, think about how you might answer the following questions:

1   How can I make sense of the information I have so far?
2   What is my intuitive reaction to the information and how can I explain this reaction?
3   What possible hypotheses explain the information?
4   What information would falsify my hypotheses?
5   What outcomes might I be seeking at this point? Why those outcomes and might anyone else in the case example be hoping for any different outcomes? If so, why?

Part 2

Following your assessment, you arrange a package of short breaks for Abigail and agree to close the case.

A year or so later, you receive a police report, informing you that El Maa has been arrested following a fight with John Jnr. A strategy meeting is held to discuss any possible risks to the children but no further action is taken. A few days after this, you find out that Talia has given birth to a baby girl, Gail, who is now a few months old. You contact El Maa to arrange another home visit but she informs you she is not feeling well and is on her way to the hospital. El Maa is seen by a psychiatrist who confirms she has a personality disorder and clinical depression. El Maa informs the psychiatrist that she has been taking anti-depressants and drinking alcohol every day. You speak to El Maa again on the phone and she says she has also been taking crack cocaine. El Maa is soon discharged from the hospital and returns home.

A day after this, Abigail is taken to hospital by El Maa with a head injury. Although the doctors feel that the injury was accidental – El Maa says Abigail fell out of bed – El Maa is very agitated with the doctors and demands various tests. El Maa is eventually escorted out of the hospital by security staff. El Maa returns home with Abigail but the next day, you receive another police report – El Maa has been arrested for assaulting John Snr. When you contact El Maa about this, she says she needs a residential detox programme and feels like no one is helping her even when she tells people her problems.

Table 6.2   Chronology

Date	Event
02/04/2009	Birth of Gail Bello
17/06/2009	Ms Bello arrested after fighting with John Jnr.
23/06/2009	Child protection strategy discussion
30/06/2009	Ms Bello self-refers to the local mental health unit
04/07/2009	Abigail taken to hospital with head injury
05/07/2009	Ms Bello arrested for assaulting John Snr.

Reflection and analysis point

At this point in the case example, again reflect back on what you know so far about Abigail and her family. You might want to consider completing one or more of the following:

- modified SWOT analysis (see p. 56)
- a basic systems analysis (see p. 59)
- an ecological-transactional analysis (see p. 65)

If you are able to complete more than one, compare the different methods and the type of analysis they provide – do they complement each other or does using a different method guide your thinking in a different way? If so, why might this be the case?

You might also want to consider completing an updated needs analysis (see p. 76) but also a decision tree (see p. 77).

Once you have completed the above tasks, think about how you might answer the following questions:

1 How can I make sense of the information I have so far?
2 What possible hypotheses explain the information?
3 What information would falsify my hypotheses?
4 How worried are you about the children in this case example? If you are worried, what are you worried about? If you are not very worried, why not?

Part 3

You make an application to your Panel to fund a residential detox programme for El Maa but this is declined because of her history of relapse. You inform El Maa of this and arrange to visit her later in the week. However, before the visit takes place, El Maa sends you a text message saying that she has taken an overdose of sleeping pills. You alert the police who attend the house and take El Maa to hospital. Abigail is accommodated into foster care. John Jnr decides that he wants to stay at home on his own (he is now 17). El-Maa remains in the mental health unit of the local hospital for a few weeks and is then discharged. El Maa declines to accept support from the community mental health team, saying her problems are with drugs and alcohol not her mental state. After a few weeks of monitoring visits, Abigail is returned home. You contact El Maa's drug and alcohol key worker who informs you that El Maa is attending a support group three times per week and she is doing well. You continue to visit Abigail at home every few weeks and remain in contact with her school and El Maa's key worker. Abigail appears to be well and her school report says she is a happy and settled young woman.

A couple of months later, you receive a phone call from El Maa. She informs you that Talia has been diagnosed with schizophrenia and that she, El Maa, has been taking heroin regularly. Abigail is accommodated into foster care. El Maa re-engages with her drug and alcohol key worker and after two months, she appears more stable and drug free. Abigail returns home. However, Talia has become very unwell and is admitted to hospital. Gail is accommodated into foster care. Talia is discharged after a few weeks but

Gail remains in foster care as Talia does not feel able to care for her. As plans are being made later for Gail to return home, the police report that Talia has been arrested for attempting to assault her partner with an axe. The plans to return Gail home are not progressed. El Maa reports taking crack cocaine and this time when you approach Panel, they do agree funding for a residential detox programme. Agreement is also given for Abigail to be accommodated for a period of six months.

Table 6.3   Chronology

Date	Event
08/08/2009	El Maa sends a text saying she has taken an overdose – Abigail accommodated in foster care
09/08/2009	El Maa admitted to local mental health unit
01/09/2009	El Maa discharged from hospital
30/09/2009	Abigail returned home
12/10/2009	Talia diagnosed with schizophrenia – El Maa reports misusing substances
13/10/2009	Abigail accommodated in foster care
29/10/2009	Talia admitted to local mental health unit. Gail accommodated in foster care
04/12/2009	Talia discharged from hospital
23/12/2009	Gail arrested for attacking her partner with an axe
23/12/2009	El Maa reports misusing substances; Abigail accommodated in foster care for six months

Reflection and analysis point

At this point in the case example, we want you to particularly think about El Maa Bello. Using the information you have so far, draw up a more detailed chronology for El Maa, using and expanding upon the two example chronologies we have provided.

Using this chronology, draw up at least two hypotheses that would explain El Maa's behaviour, as you understand it.

Once you have completed the above tasks, think about how you might answer the following questions:

1   What information, if you obtained it, would confirm each of your hypotheses?
2   What information, if you obtained it, would falsify each of your hypotheses?
3   Which of your hypotheses do you find more convincing? Why?
4   Imagine you were to share your hypotheses with El Maa. Which, if any, do you think she would find to be a reasonable explanation for her own behaviour?
5   Can you think of an alternative hypothesis that El Maa might suggest to you that explains her own behaviour (i.e. a different hypothesis from the ones you have so far thought of)? What information would confirm or disconfirm the hypothesis you think El Maa might suggest?

Part 4

Six months pass and Abigail appears to be doing well in foster care although she is keen to return home. El Maa completes her residential programme and reports of her progress are very positive. As El Maa leaves the residential programme, she agrees to engage in a three month intensive community support programme to ensure she does not regress. Gail remains in foster care and plans are in motion for her to be adopted as Talia is not responding well to treatment and is felt to remain a potential risk for her. El Maa informs you that she does feel like taking drugs again but she has given her bank cards to John Jnr so that she has no access to money. El Maa continues to attend drug and alcohol support groups but her key worker contacts you to say she is increasingly concerned. Although El Maa appears to be drug free she is 'acting strangely'. The key worker reports one session that ended when El Maa accused staff of treating her like 'a slave'. You visit El Maa and she informs you that she is pregnant. Abigail continues to present as happy and well settled. Her physical care remains excellent. You ask El Maa about accommodating Abigail but she responds coldly and asks you to leave.

After a few months, a full care order is secured for Gail and plans are accelerated for her to be adopted. El Maa informs you that she is planning to kill Gail's social worker, blaming her for breaking up her family. You inform the police, who give El Maa a warning. El Maa informs you that she plans to tell Abigail that Gail died in a car crash, so she does not wonder what happened to her niece. You discuss with El Maa the implications of such a plan and how Abigail would be affected. El Maa agrees it is not a good idea. El Maa also informs you she has had a miscarriage and has obtained her bank cards back from John Jnr. You offer to accommodate Abigail again but El Maa declines, telling you that 'you are just part of the system, you do not understand me and my plans'. Later in the week, El Maa makes another threat to kill Gail's social worker and this time the police arrest her for harassment. Abigail is accommodated into foster care and El Maa talks to you very calmly about spending the next few years in prison for what she has done. However, although a court hearing finds El Maa guilty of harassment, she is sentenced to a two-year suspended prison sentence and order to complete 200 hours of community service. Abigail remains in foster care. You visit Abigail at school and for the first time in all of the time you have known her, she appears unhappy. Abigail tells you she will not be able to see her foster carers any more as El Maa does not like them. Abigail appears quite tearful and soon changes the topic of conversation.

El Maa does not attend her first meeting with the probation service and accuses you of being part of a 'devil system'. She attends a second meeting with probation but is asked to leave as she is very agitated and accuses the probation staff of plotting to assassinate her. At around the same time, Abigail's foster carers inform you that they can no longer care for Abigail due to El Maa's increasingly belligerent and bizarre behaviour towards them. El Maa says she can no longer work with any non-black members of staff, including Abigail's foster carers (who are Arabic). You convene a child protection conference but the chair finds no reason for a child protection plan. A legal planning meeting is also held but based mainly on Abigail's presentation – which has always remained good – they advise that threshold for court proceedings has not been met.

Reflection and analysis point

At this point in the case example, we want you to consider three particular points that have arisen and try to hypothesize or explain why they might have happened. The three points are:

1   The change in El Maa's attitude towards services, from asking for help (in Part 1), to rejecting support as part of a 'devil system' (in Part 4).
2   Abigail's presentation as primarily happy and settled (Parts 1–3) and then the first sign that she might be unhappy (in Part 4)
3   John Jnr's role in the family – at times, being seen by El Maa as a source of support (e.g. holding his mother's bank cards in Part 4) and at other times not (e.g. being attacked by his mother in Part 2).

The task is to generate at least two hypotheses that would explain each of the above points. You should then seek to identify information that would confirm or disconfirm each hypothesis.

Consider completing one or more of the following, based on all the information you know so far:

1   Modified SWOT analysis
2   Basic systems analysis
3   Ecological-transactional analysis

Finally, complete a decision tree for one or more of the following people:

1   El Maa Bello
2   Abigail
3   Gail

Case example 2 – adults

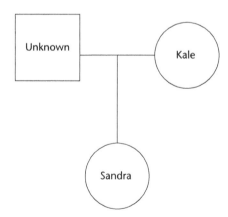

Figure 6.2   Genogram

Part 1

Table 6.4 Chronology

Date	Event
10/01/2010	Case responsibility for Sandra transferred from the Child and Adolescent Mental Health Service to the Adult Community Mental Health Team for ongoing support. The transfer summary from the children's team suggests Sandra has previously made 'threats' to 'self-harm'.
19/02/2010	Assessment completed by the Adult Community Mental Health Team – the report concludes that Sandra is at a 'low risk' but that she would benefit from ongoing therapeutic support.
13/08/2010	Call made by Kale, Sandra's mother, to the Adult Community Mental Health Team. Kale informs the team that she no longer feels able to have Sandra living with her at home.
16/08/2010	A social worker from the Adult Community Mental Health Team contacts the Housing Department on Sandra's behalf and makes an application for re-housing.
28/04/2011	A newly qualified social worker from the Adult Community Mental Health Team is allocated to Sandra.

As a new social worker in an Adult Community Mental Health Team, you have been assigned to work with Sandra, a 20-year-old young woman. Sandra's case file indicates that she is White British and that currently, she lives with her mother, Kale, in a three-bedroomed house in a relatively affluent part of the local area. Sandra's file also notes that she has been known to the local authority for eight years, since she was 12 years old. During this time, Sandra has been in and out of the care system. You read that these periods in care were all arranged with Kale's voluntary consent and that no court orders were ever sought or made. However, more recently, Sandra returned home to live with her mother and Children's Services undertook some intensive therapeutic family work to ensure that Sandra could remain at home until she was at least 18 years old. This intervention appears to have been relatively successful, certainly in the sense that it seemed to help prevent Sandra from returning into care. As you delve further into the case file, you find that although there have been plenty of assessments of Sandra and her needs, none of them seem to contain any details regarding the family history. Having said this, many of the assessments do note that Sandra does have a close relationship to her mother, albeit turbulent at times, and that this relationship is a source of strength and resilience for Sandra.

You also read that Sandra has been diagnosed with a mental illness but despite an extensive search of the records, you cannot seem to find any record of when the original diagnosis was made or by whom. You also cannot find any references to what the specific mental illness might be. You do find a clinic note written by a child psychiatrist, in which the possibility of Sandra have a learning disability is also raised. After reading the case file, you undertake two home visits to meet Sandra and, like previous social workers, you also note the apparently close relationship between Sandra and Kale. Since being allocated to Sandra, you have conducted two home visits, and like previous social workers, have noticed the close relationship between Sandra and Kale. This leads you to wonder why Kale might have given consent for Sandra to be accommodated on various occasions when she was a child and also why she has apparently decided that Sandra can no longer live at home as an adult either.

Reflection and analysis point

From your first two home visits and your reading of the case file, you decide that you do not know enough information about Sandra's family history. Inspired by an ecological-transactional approach (see p. 65), you conclude that this is a vital area to explore further.

In order to plan your work as effectively as possible, consider the following questions:

1   What specific information would you seek to obtain about Sandra's family history and why?
2   How would you go about obtaining the information? Be as specific as possible – who would you talk to and what would you ask them?
3   What might your initial hypothesis be about why Kale has voluntarily consented for Sandra to go in and out of care as a child? How does your hypothesis take account of the apparently close relationship between Sandra and Kale?

Part 2

Through your efforts to find out more about Sandra's family history, you are able to add a significant amount of information to that contained on the case file. You discover, apparently for the first time, that Sandra is Kale's adoptive daughter and that Kale and her late husband adopted Sandra when she was just a few months old. You also find out that Sandra's biological mother was mixed-heritage and her biological father was white. Kale informs you that when Sandra was first adopted, as White British adopters they did not feel that they had any real knowledge or understanding of Sandra's heritage and so they decided that they would not tell Sandra about this part of her background and simply raise her as 'white'.

As Kale tells you this information, she appears very anxious and practically begs you not to tell Sandra. Kale explains that when Sandra was a child, she deliberately kept this information from all of Sandra's social workers for fear that, as she was frequently in care, Kale would not be around to prevent Sandra from being told. You realize that this secrecy on Kale's part may well explain why there is so little information about family history on the file. Another revelation from Kale is that her late husband was abusive towards her, emotionally and physically. He was also very controlling and prevented Kale from working, partly to stop her from having financial independence but also because of his jealously that she would then meet and become friends with other people, especially other men. Kale admits that Sandra would have experienced this abuse and on several occasions, Kale is sure that

Sandra must have seen physical violence in the home. Finally, Kale informs you that she has been diagnosed with Macular Degeneration, an age-related condition which results in a loss of vision in the middle of the visual field. Kale explains that as her vision is increasingly deteriorating, she feels increasingly unable to cope with daily life.

You obtained this information from Kale over the course of several weeks. During this time, Sandra has appeared to be very settled at home. She has enrolled on a catering course as a local college and has told you of her determination to find a job after completing the course. You have also noticed that Sandra appears to take responsibility for most of the housework at home and you wonder whether this has always been the case or whether it might be related to Kale's medical condition. You also take time to visit Sandra at college and take the opportunity to speak with one of her tutors. He reports that Sandra is doing well, for the most part, but does seem to struggle to retain learning from one week to the next.

Reflection and analysis point

At this point in the case example, we want you to address two questions as follows:

1 Who cares for whom in the relationship between Sandra and Kale? How would you justify and explain your answer?
2 How does the information you now know challenge the hypothesis you formed in Part 1? If the new information does not challenge your hypothesis, can you think of any information that would?

Consider completing one or more of the following, based on the information you have now:

1 A SWOT analysis (see pp. 56–9) regarding the possibility of Sandra living independently.
2 A decision tree (see pp. 77–81) for Sandra in terms of her options for accommodation. You could also consider whether the decision tree would look any different – and how – if you completed it from Kale's perspective.

Part 3

Having updated your assessment of Sandra, you take a three-week break from work and go on a much-needed holiday. You return to find there has been a major development in the case. Sandra has been admitted to hospital under Section 3 of the Mental Health Act (1983, amended 2007) and is currently an in-patient in a psychiatric hospital. No one from your team has been able to contact Sandra or Kale and when you try and ring Kale's mobile phone, you find it is switched off and the voice mail box is full. You decide to conduct an unannounced home visit and although you think you can hear at least one person moving around inside, no one comes to answer the door when you knock and ring the doorbell. You decide to leave but on your way home from work at the end of the day, you happen to pass by the house again and decide to try one more time. After several minutes of knocking, Kale eventually answers the door but only to tell you that she does not want to talk to you or to any so-called professional any more. However, you are persistent and remind her how well you have been working together and that you only want to understand what has happened. Kale relents and invites you inside and you immediately notice how uncharacteristically untidy the house has become.

You talk with Kale and she tells you that around four months ago, she and Sandra had an explosive argument about some missing jewellery. Kale seems embarrassed when she tells you that she actually called the police and accused Sandra of having stolen the jewellery. Kale says she thinks Sandra has a drug habit. Somewhat surprised, you ask Kale to explain why she thinks this might be the case and Kale tells you that Sandra's behaviour has become somewhat unpredictable and that she has seemed lethargic and withdrawn at home but animated and 'over-stimulated' when out in the community. Kale also tells you she knows Sandra has made lots of new 'friends' at college. Kale says many of these new friends are black and that she believes they are involved in drug dealing. Sandra was arrested on suspicion of theft and bailed shortly afterwards. As she had nowhere else to go, Sandra returned home; Kale said the atmosphere in the house was very tense. You ask whether the situation was ever resolved and Kale again appears embarrassed as she tells you she later found the jewellery down the back of her dresser. Kale says it must have fallen without her noticing. Kale gives you the name of the office who arrested Sandra – PC Norman.

On your return to the office, you contact PC Norman to discuss what has happened. PC Norman informs you that she responded to a 999 call from Kale and Sandra was subsequently arrested. PC Norman confirms that Sandra was bailed the following day but when PC Norman returned a week or so later to ask Sandra to come back into the station for further questioning, Sandra became so aggressive and violent that PC Norman felt she had no choice but to take Sandra to hospital for an assessment of her mental health. PC Norman informs you that when Sandra arrived at the local hospital with the police, one of the doctors heard her threatening to kill her mother. This threat, combined with Sandra's history, led the medical professionals to conclude that Sandra did pose a risk to others and therefore, she was placed under a section for treatment.

PC Norman also mentions to you that Sandra has been arrested on several previous occasions for violent behaviour and that the police risk assessment is that Sandra is at serious risk of harming others but also of being a victim of crime. During your conversation with PC Norman, you are somewhat surprised to find out that she does not know the jewellery has been found and therefore, the investigation of Sandra for alleged theft is still active.

Reflection and analysis point

At this point in the case example, you might like to consider the following:

1 Use a basic systems approach (see pp. 59–65) and create a diagram or 'ecomap' of the various systems that Sandra operates in and how they might be connected.
2 Complete a cultural review (see pp. 74–6) of Sandra.

You might also like to consider the following questions:

1   Would your own risk assessment of Sandra differ at all from that made by the police or by the psychiatric team at the hospital? If so, why? If not, why not?

2   Kale's hypothesis for Sandra's recent change in behaviour is that she is being negatively influenced by friends at college and that she is taking drugs. Can you think of two other hypotheses that might explain Sandra's behaviour and at least one way in which each of the three hypotheses (Kale's and the two you come up with) could be falsified?

Part 4

As a next step, you arrange to visit Sandra in hospital. When you do so, Sandra appears calm and she readily informs you of the specifics of the Mental Health Act, what the guidance says professionals should and should not do and how she intends to appeal to a Tribunal to be discharged from the section.

You plan to visit Sandra again two weeks later but before this happens, Kale contacts you to tell you that Sandra is already back at home. You visit and Sandra informs you that the Tribunal found in her favour. In your discussions about her recent experiences, Sandra told you that she is 'fed up' with how people perceive her and she blames PC Norman and Kale for her being sectioned. Sandra complains that 'people think I don't understand but I know exactly what is going on'. Despite her apparent frustration at being stigmatized by the police and her successful appeal against her detention under Section, Sandra tells you that she is planning on returning to hospital voluntarily to seek 'treatment for depression and learning disability'.

Table 6.5 Chronology

Date	Event
02/06/2011	Updated assessment completed.
09/06/2011	Sandra arrested on suspicions of theft.
10/06/2011	Sandra released on bail.
16/06/2011	Sandra admitted to hospital under section 3 of the Mental Health Act (1983, amended 2007).
01/07/2011	Mental Health Tribunal discharges Sandra's section and she leaves the hospital.

Summary and conclusions

As indicated in the Introduction, we hope that these two in-depth case examples have allowed you to practise with the tools, models and ideas discussed in the book so far. Clearly, as with any case example, there is a temptation to say 'we would need more information' or 'that is not what I would have done in that situation'. These are valid points, to a certain extent, but equally we think it is important that you do not use these kinds of statements as a way of overlooking what is contained within the case examples. If you do feel you would have done something differently or obtained different information, it can be helpful to be as specific as possible – what would you have done and why? What do you think would have happened? What information would you want, from whom and how you would obtain it?

The scenarios presented here – about El Maa and her children, Sandra and Kale – show how analysis needs to be an ongoing process and not just a one-off event. As a matter of good practice, we need to become used to revaluating our previous hypothesis and judgements. New information and developments should be prompts for practitioners to engage in fresh analytical thinking rather than only being absorbed into current ways of understanding.

We also believe that the case examples of El Maa, Sandra and Kale show how critical analysis requires more than a theoretical understanding of service users' situations. This highlights one of the key themes of the book: that critical case analysis is the foundation of good practice and is based not only on accumulating information but on taking – without being flippant – a 'playful' approach to seeing how different pieces of information might be more or less important, how different pieces of information might be viewed from a variety of perspectives and how the real lives of services users (and indeed, of anyone if you cared to look closely enough) are so complex as to make discussions about the absolute 'right' or 'wrong' thing to do irrelevant. Instead, we need to learn to think more in terms of making better decisions based on the information we currently have. This approach makes it far easier to change your mind about a situation or service user without feeling this must mean your previous view was 'wrong'. Rather, your view at any one time should be seen as the best approximation available based on a thorough analysis of the information currently known.

Finally, if you have attempted to complete these case examples on your own, you may well have found it quite difficult to think about issues such as multiple hypotheses and where you may have been 'guilty' of confirmation bias. If this is the case, as we have stressed elsewhere, please do not worry too much. Thinking about complex situations such as those presented in these case examples is generally easier when you have at least one other colleague or manager to assist you. If you have only been able to so far consider these case examples on your own, it may be helpful to think about discussing all or part of one of them in a team meeting or in your next supervision. If you do plan to do so, the next chapter may be especially helpful as we discuss the role of supervision in critical analysis.

Key points from this chapter include

- A key aspect of critical analysis involves an awareness of significant developments in service users' lives.
- New information or developments should be seen as opportunities to engage in fresh critical analysis.
- Practice should be predicated on making better rather than worse decisions and not on absolutes of right or wrong.
- Changing your mind based on new information or a fresh critical analysis of a case is often the sign of a confident, analytically minded practitioner and hence should be seen as a strength rather than a weakness in practice.

Recommended reading

Brayne, H. and Carr, H. (2010) *Law for Social Workers*, 11th revised edition. Oxford: Oxford University Press.

Dalzell, R. and Sawyer, E. (2011) *Putting Analysis into Assessment: Undertaking Assessments of Need – A Toolkit for Practitioners*, 2nd revised edition. London: National Children's Bureau Limited.

Research in Practice (2009) *Analysis and Critical Thinking in Assessment*. Sheffield: Research in Practice.

7 Supervision, reflection and critical analysis

Chapter overview

By the end of this chapter, you should understand:

- The meaning and role of supervision for critical analysis
- How to distinguish between formal and informal models of supervision
- The central role of supervision to good practice
- How supervision can be used as a 'space' for critical analysis

Introduction

In this chapter we examine how practitioners can use supervision as a space for critical analysis. As we have discussed elsewhere in the book, supervision is one of the best places for practitioners to engage in critical analytical thinking, making use of the supervisory relationship to check out their ideas, generate different hypotheses and challenge biases. To this end, we start the chapter by reviewing various definitions and exploring some different models of supervision.

In social work and other literature, supervision is typically seen as a means by which organizations, such as local authorities, can hold practitioners to account as well as a way of imparting new knowledge to them. Supervision can be 'formal' and if so, will tend to focus on 'case work' – however, supervision can also be based on themes, as opposed to case work, and can also take place in a group rather than just with one practitioner and one manager. We will explain and discuss these different approaches as well as considering the role of 'informal' supervision (Pawson et al. 2003). After this discussion, which we think will help to highlight the complexity of supervision, we conclude the chapter by offering some tips and ideas on how to get the most out of supervision, whether as a manager or as a practitioner.

The meaning of supervision

In their review of the literature, Bogo and McKnight (2006: 55) describe supervision as:

> a primary vehicle through which agency accountability is achieved. Supervisors, often located at mid-level in the organization's hierarchy, oversee the work of front-line staff as they carry out the mandate and purpose of an organization. The importance of education and support of workers has also been well recognized as a crucial aspect of supervision that contributes to effective practice.

Although we dislike the language of 'front-line' staff (which conjures up – in our minds at least – a military analogy), the implication of this definition is that supervision is *required* in order for practitioners to carry out their roles. In other words, supervision is not an optional extra to practice but a key component of it. This leads to the conclusion that supervision is – or should be – far more than simply a meeting between a practitioner and a manager to discuss a series of 'cases'. Bogo and McKnight discuss three main aspects of supervision that go beyond case work (see Kadushin and Harkness 2002):

1 *Educational* Educational supervision is the part of supervision in which practitioners are given information in order to perform their role more effectively – this would include information about the duties of their agency, available resources and policies and procedures. This could also be information about changing national legislation but also about the practitioner's individual training needs.

2 *Administrative* Administrative supervision is the part of supervision in which managers monitor the performance of practitioners, especially with regards to the completion of tasks (on time, hopefully!) and the requirements of their job description. Seen in this way, supervision is perhaps the main way through which agencies such as local authorities ensure the accountability of practitioners.

3 *Supportive* Finally, supportive supervision is that which aims to assist practitioners in managing personal stress and as a way of helping practitioners process and take account of their emotional and intuitive thoughts and feelings. According to Bogo and McKnight (citing Kadushin and Harkness 2002), supportive supervision is achieved by supervisors 'providing encouragement, reassurance, and [enabling] appropriate autonomy' (Kadushin and Harkness 2002). 'It [supportive supervision] is concerned with enhancing staff morale and job satisfaction of social workers' (Bogo and McKnight 2006: 52).

By referring to these three 'types' of supervision – educational, administrative and supportive – we hope to begin to highlight the complexity of the supervisory relationship as well as pointing towards the power differential inherent within supervision. Formal supervision is based upon an organizational hierarchy in which managers supervise less senior practitioners and can lead to a view in which managers have less to learn from practitioners than practitioners have to learn from managers. This is not a view of supervision that we find particularly helpful when thinking about critical analysis.

Moreover, such a view of supervision as organizational and purely formal can lead to practitioners feeling less powerful and disinclined to challenge any perceived unfairness; what may seem on the surface to be an equal relationship between supervisor and supervisee can in fact be a very unequal power relationship, affected by complex ideas such as class, gender, race and disability. It is interesting to consider how this aspect of supervision can mirror the relationship between practitioners and service users – what can appear to be a benign and equal relationship between a service user and a practitioner can often feel quite different to the service user (see Tew 2005, for an interesting discussion of power relations in social work).

Although managers clearly do have power through their organizational positions, it is possible to deploy this power more ethically in supervision by constructively challenging practitioners' decisions and allowing practitioners to do the same with regards to managers' decisions. Indeed, one way in which practitioners can be said to have 'an advantage' in this is via their direct work with service users, something that will much less often apply to the manager. Through supervision, practitioners are well positioned to inform their managers of potentially better ways of meeting service users' needs. Seen in this way, managers have as much to learn from practitioners, if not more, than vice versa (Gould and Baldwin 2004). This challenges the view of supervision as being a process in which managers are experts, having a form of 'super' vision that somehow allows them to make better decisions than practitioners.

Models of supervision

Formal case work

The complexity of supervision and the power dynamics within it can complicate the status of supervision as being a safe space in which to talk and reflect and to analyse. A purely casework model of supervision can also detract from this.

The casework model of supervision is one in which the educational, administrative and supportive aspects of supervision are linked primarily, if not entirely, to the discussion of individual service users or 'cases'. This is likely to be the model that most qualified practitioners are used to (see Tsui 2005). Using the casework model, practitioners will be asked to talk about their 'case work', about the tasks they have completed (or not) and to make an action plan for the near future. As Tsui notes, despite its widespread usage, this model is actually best suited for less experienced practitioners; ideally, over time, as the practitioner's experience and confidence grow, the nature of supervision should change with it and develop to become less focused on tasks and more on themes, on reflection and on critical analysis.

One way of understanding your own supervisory needs is through a level of self-reflection about what you actually need from your supervision. This requires you to be an active participant rather than passively accepting whatever supervision is on offer.

We end this section by noting that while the casework model is based on a one-to-one relationship, group supervision especially seems to offer a better way of ensuring critical and analytical practice.

Group supervision

Kadushin and Harkness (2002) define group supervision as: 'the use of a group setting to implement . . . supervision. In group supervision, the supervisor . . . meets with the group to discharge [his or her] responsibilities [and supervision] is implemented in the group and through the group' (p. 390). Kadushin and Harkness see many advantages to group supervision. Not only can group supervision be more efficient – several practitioners can receive supervision at the same time – but having more people in supervision at the same time inevitably brings more and different experiences. This means that a variety of practice situations and experiences can be discussed and, in all likelihood, more options, solutions, hypothesis – in short, more critical analysis – can take place than when discussing something between only two people. Our view is that it is very much a case of more cooks helping the broth rather than spoiling it (although, of course, there are limits to this, as with any discursive meeting).

Despite these advantages, group supervision appears to be rarely used in statutory settings, probably because practitioners are thought of as having individual learning and emotional needs but also because of the focus on accountability and performance.

Informal supervision

Informal supervision can be understood as any supervision that takes place outside of formal settings but which still has the 'aim' or outcome of providing practitioners with a space to discuss, reflect, analyse and obtain guidance on their practice (Carson et al. 2011). Informal supervision can therefore occur in team meetings, in discussions with colleagues and in interactions with service users. This last aspect of supervision is often overlooked – can service users really be involved in supervision? We would argue they can, if by supervision we mean a forum or process for thinking more deeply about a service user and their situation. As we have argued in Chapter 3, service users should not be excluded from a critical analysis of their own situations and indeed, by seeing service users only as providers of information, much of the value of genuine partnership working can be lost.

One potential advantage of informal supervision is that it can often feel less constrained by the need to follow a fixed agenda or take detailed notes. Clearly, supervision does need to be recorded both for individual practitioners and on service users' files but this becomes more complicated when one considers the nuances and complexity of supervision and compares this with the types of electronic recording systems most practitioners will be used to.

Studies have shown that the electronic forms of recording that have increasingly come to dominate modern practice do not capture or recognize the subtleties of social work. We would go further and argue that they *cannot* do so, even were they to be substantially redesigned. White et al. (2008) have shown that in children's services especially, the design of electronic forms restricts the narratives that practitioners are able to tell about service users and their needs (see the Introduction for our discussion of the importance of narratives). Similarly, Broadhurst et al. (2010) show that due to the 'one-size-fits-all' design of social work electronic systems, practitioners often end up having to juggle the demands of electronic forms with their actual views of the reality of service users' lives. Broadhurst et al. rightly note that especially the delicacy and complexity of home visits can get lost in what is written down afterwards.

Another difficulty with electronic records is the difficulty of recording intuition (Zeira and Rosen 2000). As discussed in Chapter 3, intuitive knowledge is by definition not easy to articulate verbally, let alone in written form. As Pawson et al. have argued, 'practitioners may make selective observations on a case, and then go through a personal and experientially based archive of patterns and experiences to arrive at a chosen course of action' (2003: 52).

Intuitive knowledge is often gained from personal reflections and experiences that are hard to document. They may be remembered spontaneously, sometimes even outside the context of the present conversation. Informal supervision may be a more successful way of enabling practitioners and managers to think and talk about intuitive knowledge. This is because informal supervision may often feel more 'natural' and so aid the process of unlocking or unpicking intuitive thought processes (see Shier and Graham 2011).

Guidance on supervision

The Children's Workforce Development Council (CWDC) and Skills for Care (2007) have produced comprehensive guidance on social work supervision. This guidance suggests that supervision is so critical to practice that each organization should have a published supervision policy, setting out frequency and duration but also, more importantly, the purpose of supervision. The CWDC and Skills for Care guidance aims to explain how practitioners can best use supervision as an arena for critical analysis and not simply as a method for keeping managers abreast of case development and case work. In order to effectively utilize this guidance, we feel that practitioners need to engage in a level of self-reflection so as to understand more effectively what they need from supervision and how to get it.

In what follows, we provide just two basic suggestions for practitioners to ensure they get the most from their supervision:

First, ensure that you have frequent supervision. Where supervision is infrequent, one obvious remedy is to speak with your manager and, if necessary, put something in writing to them, perhaps via email. Recently, the British Association of Social Workers asked social workers about their experiences of supervision and they found that while the majority had supervision every month, about one in ten practitioners reported never having had supervision (British Association of Social Workers 2011). This is clearly unsatisfactory – and worrying – and social workers faced with similar experiences may need to seek advice from their human resources department, perhaps informally in the first instance.

Second, keeping some of your own notes during supervision is useful, even if your manager takes primary responsibility for record keeping. It is also useful to prepare before supervision, noting down particular issues or topics you wish to discuss and questions you may which to ask. This type of preparation is similar in nature to that which you will be used to undertaking prior to a formal assessment or first home visit, being clear about the information you want, the questions you need answered and areas you need to cover. As Rowlings (1995: 75) observes 'Good supervisory relationships do not simply exist. They are working relationships which develop over time [and] what is achieved is the result of the contributions of both supervisor and supervisee.'

Reflection point: questions to consider

- From whom do you get supervision? To whom do you give supervision (especially if you are not a manager)?
- How do you prepare for supervision?
- When has supervision gone well for you and when has it gone badly?
- Can you reflect on the differences between any times when supervision has gone well and when it has gone badly?
- If supervision is not going well for you, whose responsibility is that? What might you do to improve it?
- Does it matter if every form of supervision is not fully recorded on the case file? If yes, why? If no, why not?

Supervision: critical analysis and reflection

In the remainder of the chapter, we will focus on how supervision in particular can be used as a forum or tool to aid critical analysis. Many of the tools we discussed in Chapter 5 can be used in supervision and we would encourage you to think of supervision as something not so distinct from the rest of your practice that wholly new or different tools are required. However, as we also discussed in Chapter 5, a truly analytically minded practitioner would not necessarily make formal use of such tools on each and every occasion but would rather use the tools as a way of becoming more used to thinking in particular ways. The further ideas and prompts we discuss here should be viewed in a similar way.

We will start with a practice example.

Practice example: Anita

A social worker on duty in a Referral and Assessment team receives a referral from the police informing them that Anita, a 15-year-old Black woman, is in their custody. The police report that Anita was found in a home the police raided this morning; the raid was conducted based on intelligence that the people living in the house were in the UK illegally. When Anita was asked about her relationship to the other residents, she called one of them 'uncle' but also said that they were not actually related. The police suspect that Anita may have been 'trafficked' and ask that the Referral and Assessment Team find her an emergency foster placement while the UK Border Agency arrange to deport her from the UK.

Such a referral could be dealt with quite simply in that the request of the police for a placement could be responded to – either by finding a placement or not. The supervision of this event could also be dealt with quite simply – the manager could check whether the task was complete, whether all of the required looked after children records were complete and whether this had all been done in a timely manner. This would then be a good example of casework supervision. However, such an approach would be one in which many of the assumptions inherent in this response went unexamined. Brookfield (2009) has identified some useful questions or steps that you could ask regarding assumptions and critical analysis and we suggest that these could form part of a supervision discussion (Brookfield's model is somewhat similar to the cultural review we discussed in Chapter 5 – see pp. 74–6).

Brookfield outlines four steps as follows:

1   Identify inherent assumptions.
2   Understand why these assumptions have developed and why they have been thought worthwhile.
3   Think about the assumptions from a different perspective, or imagine what a different person in a different situation would think about the assumptions.
4   Having become aware of the assumptions we have made, consider whether acting or thinking differently is now required.

Practice example: Anita

Using Brookfield's four-step model, one could debate Anita's situation in supervision by asking such questions as:

*   Is Anita to be considered primarily a victim or a potential criminal?
*   Is the relationship between Anita and her 'uncle' somehow sinister or might 'uncle' mean something different to Anita than it means to the worker?
*   Where do we imagine Anita is from? How does our view of her country of origin affect our response to her situation?

Using this relatively simple approach, it is possible – indeed, likely – that Anita would receive a better service than simply being placed in temporary care (although this is not to say there is anything wrong with Anita being placed into care – based on the information we have, it appears to be the only option). It is also likely that Anita would not only receive a better service but she would also report greater satisfaction with it were the supervision of her situation to be client focused rather than task focused (see Harkness and Hensley 1991). This example is clearly based on a one-to-one supervisory model – in the next section, we look at an example of a successful implementation of a group supervision model in one particular agency.

A model of group supervision

Both of us have previously been involved in running group supervision sessions for a local authority social work team. Group supervision is unlikely to replace one-to-one supervision – and nor should it, especially in organizations such as local authorities – but group supervision can play a complementary role. In this particular agency, we arranged for the social workers to meet together as a group, once or twice a month, to discuss 'practice' issues. These meetings took place in addition to the more businesslike team meetings and in addition to one-to-one supervisions with line managers. They provided a forum to discuss broader practice themes rather than focusing on individual service users. As this group supervision took place in a disabled children's team, we focused on issues or themes such as communicating with disabled children, disabled children and child protection, on parental experiences of caring for a disabled child and so on. On occasion, we would invite outside speakers to attend the meetings – on one occasion, we invited a group of parents of disabled children to talk to us about their experiences of being assessed. These forums gave the practitioners a space to think more widely than they generally would in their more formal, casework supervision. These types of meetings need not take up a great deal of time – our meetings in this agency usually lasted for around 45 minutes to an hour.

Practice example: group supervision

As an example, in one of these group supervision sessions, we discussed the issue of assessments and how a robust social history can help inform critical analysis. We did this by providing the practitioners with a brief extract from *Analysing Childhood Deaths and Serious Injury Through Abuse and Neglect: What can we Learn? A Biennial Analysis of Serious Case Reviews 2003–2005* (Brandon et al. 2008) as follows:

> One of the key bits of information that helps frame (an) understanding of parent-child interaction, children's . . . development, and children's care and protection is the carer's state of mind.
>
> [The carer's state of mind] is the product of a long history of developmental transactions, the broad trajectory of which is launched by the caregiver's own experiences of being cared for, protected, and understood or not by his or her own parents. Caregiver states of mind can therefore be understood in terms of the parent's relationship history and current patterns of interaction with children, partners, peers, professionals.
>
> Reder and Duncan (1999, p. 22) argued that an important omission from the majority of files was information about the personal and family histories of the parents [and this] restricted our ability to make sense of their relationship with other adults and with their children.
>
> In many cases, it was all too common for agencies and assessors to 'describe' their way around the three sides of the Assessment Framework without properly generating an analysis.

Essentially, what this extract is saying is that when assessing a child who may be at risk of harm, one of the key bits of information is a robust and detailed history of the parent(s) but that this is often missing.

We gave the practitioners a chance to read and digest this extract and then we asked them to consider whether this had any resonance for the service users they were currently working with. We asked them to think about the following questions or reflection points and to discuss them in pairs before feeding back to the group:

- Think about a child and family you have worked with where you have been frustrated by – or lack an understand of – why the parent behaves in the way they do or why they cannot parent differently.
- Briefly describe the situation to your colleague and see how far you can explain any of the following:
  - the parent's early experiences of relationships and of being cared for;
  - the parent's current views of themselves, their partner and/or their own parents;
  - their parenting behaviour;
  - their child's daily experiences of being cared for.
- If you find that you cannot tell your colleague much about these issues, think about how you might find out and whether it would help inform your assessments.

We then asked them to think about how they might gather this information:

- Would you ask the parent questions – if so, what questions?
- Would you ask the child questions – if so, what questions?
- Would you aim to observe the parent and child together – if so, what would you be looking for?
- Would you want information from other professionals or family members – if so, who and what questions would you ask them?

In this way, we aimed to help the practitioners think about a broad theme – in this case, the importance of a robust and detailed social and relational history – and then to relate it to an individual child and family.

In a small group (at least three people), you could work through the plan set out above. Read the extract together and then think about an individual service user about whom you are worried. Think about the questions and reflection points we have laid out.

Supervision that requires critical thought

In addition to the Brookfield model above and the tools in Chapter 5, we would hope by now that readers who have progressed through the book sequentially will understand that our whole purpose has been to encourage an analytically minded approach to practice. Bearing this in mind, our final suggestion for supervision is to think of it as a model of the way you practise with service users. Supervision can offer a safe space to practise how you might address a particular issue with a service user, to consider your emotional and intuitive responses and to take note and account of these before they 'surprise' you at a later date. Our view is that if practitioners (or their managers) cannot use supervision as an open, exploratory process of give-and-take then this would worry us about how they could form an open, exploratory, give-and-take relationship with service users.

While the following prompts and questions are not exactly a model to follow, we think they are the kind of more useful questions that could be asked and discussed in supervision. Once you get used to these kinds of questions, supervision should become a far more productive and client-centred process although we should warn you, it will also become a more challenging process for you as a practitioner (see the Introduction where we discuss how hard, mental effort is similar in many ways to hard, physical effort).

Practice example

Try using the following questions and prompts as part of your supervision:

Decision-making

- Be explicit about the steps that led up to the decision.
- What were the alternatives and why were they rejected?
- What assumptions might have contributed to the decision that was made?

Direct work with service users

- What are the potential benefits of adopting a more 'confrontational' or supportive approach with this service user?
- How does the service user make you feel and why?
- How well do you understand what life is like for this service user?
- What are the service user's views on what is happening? If you do not know, how will you find out? If you do know, what are you going to do about their views?
- What would the service user notice is different now from before you started working with them?

Risk

- How explicitly can you describe the risk to the service user?
- Spelling it out step by step, what is the (plausible) worst case scenario that you think might happen?
- How likely is the worst case scenario and what would make it less likely?
- Who is responsible for causing the risk to the service user and how?
- In as much detail as you can, what steps have you taken or will you take to reduce the risk?
- How will the steps you plan to take actually make a difference?

Summary and conclusions

In this penultimate chapter, we have tried to demonstrate both how fundamental supervision is to good practice but also how complex a relationship the supervisory one often is. We have discussed how supervision has a wider meaning than simply being about one practitioner and one manager having a formal and set meeting together to discuss casework. Supervision happens far more dynamically and with more fluidity than this, even if this is not always recognized. We have also highlighted our belief in the value of group supervision as a complementary process to one-to-one supervision. Using practice examples and exercises, we hope we have given you some ideas, whether you are a practitioner or a manager, on how to make your supervision require – and prompt – more critical analysis.

Recommended reading

D'Cruz, H., Gillingham, P. and Melendez, S. (2007) Reflexivity, its meanings and relevance for social work: a critical review of the literature, *British Journal of Social Work*, 37(1): 73–90.

Children's Workforce Development Council and Skills for Care (2007) *Providing Effective Supervision. A Workforce Development Tool*. London: CWDW and Skills for Care.

8 Conclusion

Introduction

The aim of this chapter is to reinforce the central argument of this book, namely that critical analysis can and should be incorporated into all aspects of your practice through the development of an analytical mindset. To this end, we show how the skills and knowledge that practitioners require for critical analysis, as discussed in the previous chapters, can be enhanced through regular application. We accomplish the aim of this chapter by reflecting on our own practice experiences, where necessary. Our motivation for writing this book stems from our experiences as social workers: we know that due to busy work loads, IT systems which are configured to primarily collect and store data (instead of synthesize information; Broadhurst et al. 2010), and the emotional turbulence of practice, practice can often feel – and be – reactionary, instead of analytical.

In our experience, there is much that is commendable and analytical about current social work practice, even in the face of uncertainty. However, it is not always clear from reading case files that this is the case. For example, many decisions seem to be arbitrary, suddenly appearing on a case file without apparently having been much discussed or debated beforehand. This is partly because certain decisions are reached via informal interactions between practitioners, service users and managers. In this respect, our call for practitioners to develop an analytical mindset is a call for practitioners to demonstrate more openly how decisions have been reached. For example, if a referral is not being actioned, rather than simply record this decision, one has to show what information has been taken into account to arrive at said decision, and the reasons why. In other words, demonstrating an analytical mindset can be as simple as practitioners evidencing more thoroughly the skills they use already in their practice.

At the same time, any discussion about the apparent absence of critical analysis from practice has to recognize that are also inherent problems. As a starting point, we may see critical analysis as *making sense* of pieces of information but this raises the question of quality: when is this *making-sense-of* good enough? This issue may also be seen as the problem of identification – even when we provide a definition of critical analysis, as we did in the Introduction and more fully in Chapter 1, how can we tell when it has occurred in sufficient depth? In one sense, we may have to accept that critical analysis has a retrospective quality because of the issues of definition and identification: you can only put your finger on it after evaluating the quality of professional conduct; however, evaluators usually have the benefit of hindsight and time. A more positive take may require us to sidestep the issue of definition and identification and turn our focus instead to the contexts that make quality critical analysis easier or more likely to occur (Helm 2009). In talking about contexts, we have to start with ourselves and then look outwards towards the organizations we work in.

Contexts of critical analysis

Personal

Pithouse (1998) has argued that social work practice is an ' "invisible" trade, in that it cannot be "seen" without engaging in the workers' own routine for understanding' (p. 4). Developing this idea a bit further, Pithouse suggests that this is the case because 'practitioners do not typically retrieve and analyse . . . their endeavours. Like most of us they rely upon rarely stated motives and taken for granted assumptions in order to accomplish day to day routines' (p. 5). What this means is that making critical analysis more visible and obvious in our practices requires us to *think differently* about the task at hand.

As we have argued throughout the book, thinking differently requires us to reconceptualize critical analysis as intrinsic to all aspects of practice as opposed to viewing it as a discrete part in a linear process of intervention. Typically, analysis has been considered as one of the final stages of the social work assessment process. But we have argued that analysis should be incorporated into all aspects of social work. The quotes from Pithouse above support our view that critical analysis cannot be simply an add-on to your practice (as implied by much of the official guidance) but that it is a central quality of good practice. We must recognize that, properly undertaken and applied, the process of critical analysis has the potential to make us all better practitioners because, primarily, it has the potential to lead to better outcomes for service users.

But what does this mean? Usually a referral is not considered as a 'case' until some form of initial assessment has been completed and the identified actions 'allocated' to a practitioner. It is true that practitioners 'do' some analysis even when receiving referrals; however, there is a sense that the 'real' business of social work only starts with case allocation, as such a decision indicates that the 'issues' have been considered as complex or serious enough to warrant some form of intervention, however short lived this may be in practice. Yet as we showed in Chapter 4 and elsewhere, even at the stage of the first assessment and before, through critical analysis, practitioners can 'intervene', saving time and resources. Once seen as an intrinsic part of every aspect of practice, critical analysis loses its somewhat mythical status (Helm 2009) as a desirable yet somehow elusive part of our work. Influenced by the conviction that critical analysis is essential to sound practice, our motivation in this book has been to present models, tools and ideas that will convince and enable practitioners to engage in critical analysis on a more routine basis.

We suggest that in order to incorporate critical analysis into practice, we need to reflect on the kinds of practitioners we are, as well as conduct an open audit of our skills.

In Chapters 5 and 7, we discussed cultural reviews and Brookfield's model of reflection respectively, both of which can be useful starting points for understanding ourselves (as well as service users). Through a cultural review, we pay attention to Pithouse's observation that practitioners use taken for granted assumptions. As we explored in Chapter 2 when discussing hypothesizing, as human beings, we all tend to intuitively seek information to confirm rather than refute our assumptions; accordingly, a cultural review is one way of bringing the unconscious to the fore and exposing them to challenge from new information. Brookfield's model, on the other hand, draws our attention to our 'comfort zones of practice' and by making these known, helps us to acknowledge aspects of our practice that would practically need to change in order to achieve a more analytically minded approach.

In our opinion, a 'self-audit' should also include reflecting on – and thinking differently about – our responses to the emotions that service users and the demands of our role evoke in us. Despite an acknowledgement that emotional connections with service users can lead to positive outcomes (Ruch et al. 2010), the tools for assessing need and risk in practice seem to pay scant attention to the role of emotion. The drawback about this silence is amplified when it comes to individual practitioners, where it is assumed that those who display any emotions in the workplace are incompetent or perhaps unfortunately incapable of handling the stresses of practice (Morrison 2007). However, as we have argued in Chapter 3, emotions need not be seen as 'irrational': they can be the basis of good practice if acknowledged within a sound framework of critical analysis. The change in mind-set that we argue for is one where emotions (and intuition) are viewed positively: practitioners must learn to become comfortable with asking themselves why certain feelings have been evoked and to understand the answers to these questions as another potentially relevant piece of information for use in critical analysis.

Staying with self-reflection, there are skills required for critical analysis that can be learned and as we argued in Chapter 2, similar to most relatively complex skills, critical analysis and the related skills need to be achieved through practice. For this present discussion, we use hypothesizing and research mindedness as an illustration of some of the skills required for critical analysis. Although these skills are indispensable for critical analysis, many practitioners view them as belonging more to the domain of academia than practice (Beddoe 2011) and for this reason, we revisit some themes from Chapter 2.

Skills of hypothesizing and research-mindedness

Hypothesizing involves generating reasons for *why* an event has occurred and finding evidence within available information to *refute* those reasons. Apart from its reputation as 'academic', in our experience, practitioners often do not engage in explicit hypothesizing, perhaps because it feels counter-intuitive to seek explanations for why something might not be the case. Second, employers have procedures and 'modus operandi' which are (often) well publicized but there are also ways of doing things which are tacit and informal. For instance, how an agency responds to a referral is laid out in statutory guidance and agency procedures. On the other hand, practitioners know from their routine duties and informal exchanges with colleagues about the sorts of issues – for example welfare 'dependency' – that are less likely to be viewed with favour by fellow professionals and managers (Ellis 2004). Thus, apart from feeling counter-intuitive, finding evidence to refute our initial thoughts about an event seems unnecessary, because we believe that we can tell from experience the trajectory of certain types of 'cases' (or referrals).

Our argument that critical analysis is a skill that can be practised is therefore a call for practitioners to reflect on our propensity to act intuitively; and building on this awareness, to *self-consciously* challenge our taken for granted (or day-to-day or common-sense) knowledge. Applied to referrals, the latter point means that practitioners must follow the dictum that 'every case is new' and by implication involves different people we have not (yet) encountered who will have had life experiences we do (yet) not know about. Pressed further, while we work with people, every engagement is an opportunity for our hypotheses to be refuted: in essence, to review cases at the first available opportunity and on an ongoing basis after that.

Another skill for critical analysis is the use of research knowledge. In general, many practitioners feel some ambivalence towards research: while research knowledge is highly thought of, practitioners tend to believe that academics have different priorities and identities than they do (Mitchell et al. 2009). In other words, practitioners see conducting or using research knowledge as almost exclusively the domain of academics. Notwithstanding this ambivalence, practitioners also draw on complex theories in their work, sometimes even surprising themselves with their use of sophisticated theoretical knowledge (Gordon et al. 2009). Therefore, in the case of research knowledge, both a change in mind-set and practice are required. Practitioners need to be confident that it is legitimate to evidence the use of research knowledge in their daily work. We recognize that practitioners may not always know the intricacies of the theory informing their practice. An example of this might be when a practitioner argues that a young child needs to be removed from their birth family as soon as possible and placed in a long-term foster or adoptive placement while they are still young. There are various theories and research evidence that could be used to support such a view but even if the practitioner is not aware of them, there is nevertheless much merit in spelling out – perhaps via a court statement – that this view is based upon the view that children need stability, that the earlier children are placed with families the better they tend to do and so on. Such transparency about the ideas that practitioners are drawing upon can at the very least foster debates within teams and between professionals.

Keeping to the theme of research (and theoretical) knowledge, in Chapter 4, we discussed four approaches for analysis – SWOT, a basic systems approach, an ecological-transactional approach and psychosocial approaches. Although not discussed explicitly in that chapter, we are mindful of White's (2009: 226–30) caution against 'take-away knowledge', whereby complex theories become simplified to such an extent that their potentially valuable nuances and contestable foundations are lost. As White wryly cautions

> When we add supple theory to our innate equipment for making emotional judgements and our tendencies as information processors towards seeking to

confirm our initial hypotheses (Kahneman et al., 1982), we have an intoxi-
cating concoction rendering us dizzy and drunk on our own convictions.

(White 2009: 229–30)

White is arguing that a simplistic understanding of theory or research can easily
lead to further confirmation bias in our practice.

Adding to White's warning, we restate our point in the introduction to Chapter 4,
that the four approaches discussed cannot be applied in a rigid way, and the models
have their weaknesses and strengths. An advantage of distilling the four approaches
into their key tenets – as we have done in Chapter 4 – is pragmatism, in that practitioners can 'instrumentalize' the ideas from the chapter to *make sense* of complex practice situations. Consequently, it is not the coherence or elegance of the four approaches
that matters but the kinds of cases that they can be utilized in.

White's argument is also a call for social workers to exercise judgement in their
selection of theory and research knowledge and while judgement appears to be an individual characteristic, a closer inspection shows that it can be improved through 'doing'.
Unsurprisingly, research with Scottish social workers suggests that more experienced
practitioners exercise more sound judgement (Collins and Daly 2011). We would add
that it is only by 'doing' critical analysis can practitioners reasonably hope or expect to
improve their judgement. Reflecting regularly on who we are and our biases, taking
time to think about service users, *writing* down our train of thought and seeking information from other sources to refute our intuitions and help us explain (or understand)
a situation; these are all likely to lead to better judgements even though no one can
guarantee that outcomes will therefore be uniformly positive.

Organizational – overcoming a difficult terrain

Reflecting on our own practice experiences, we know that organizational context in
social work is one of regular change. In addition to relatively high staff turnover (albeit
this problem has improved, not least because of the recession of 2008 onwards) and
frequent modifications to procedures and organizational 'restructuring', ICT systems
can actively impede critical analysis because information is held in separate places on
computer systems. Besides, the requirement to collect and input data on long electronic
forms can distract practitioners' focus from the information they actually need rather
than that demanded by the form. Moreover, the move towards multidisciplinary practice, while helpful in many, many ways, can also impede critical analysis in certain
instances because information is spread across wider professional networks. In the
current climate of public expenditure cuts, thresholds for intervention are generally
increasing across the public sector and consequently, practitioners are under (even)
more pressure to ration resources. Although the issues discussed here are well rehearsed
in the literature, current evidence suggests that they have crystallized to place practitioners under severe pressure: 'caseloads are far too high [. . .] It's a matter of crisis
management on a daily basis' (Professional Social Work 2012: 7). The difficult organization terrain discussed here only serves to illustrate the urgent need to incorporate
critical analysis in all aspects of practice. Now more than ever, thinking creatively to

understand and resolve service users' needs, skilful practice and good peer support are required to fulfil our duty to improve service users' lives.

A final thought

We have concentrated in this book almost exclusively on the issue of critical analysis but we want to conclude with a more general observation. We must both confess to a sense of nervousness about social work at present and about the profession's future. We do not pretend to have a unique insight in this regard but although there is much to be said for the focus on child protection social work (especially following the publication of the Munro report) and on moves in adult service towards individual budgets, we must not forget that children's social work is far broader than 'just' child protection and that social work with adults has historically had a far broader role than simply case management and financial assessments. Our worry is that as the squeeze on public sector spending continues, unless we as a profession can explain our unique role with service users, the possibility increases that questions will be raised about why local authorities, especially, seem to spend so much money on us. Although this may seem like a relatively pessimistic note to end the book on, let us also say that we do believe that many within the profession – and friends of the profession – are currently making this case and eloquently so. We hope that those in power will listen.

Appendix 1
Exercise 1 Cognitive reflection test: the most common answers

1   Intuitive answer – 100 minutes
    Rational answer – 5 minutes
2   Intuitive answer – 24 days
    Rational answer – 47 days
3   Intuitive answer – 10 pence
    Rational answer – 5 pence.

We will leave you to work out which answers are actually correct for yourselves!

Appendix 2
Exercise 2 What outcomes?

1   What outcomes do you think Angie's parents might want from the referral?

   For Angie to be safe; for Angie to listen to them and obey their rules; for Angie to be protected from the influence of drugs; for Angie to realize that she is a vulnerable adult.

2   What outcomes do you think Angie might want from the referral, if any?

   For her parents to stop treating her like a child; to be allowed to choose her own friends; to be supported to live in her community; for someone to ask her opinion and views on the situation.

3   What outcomes would you, as a social worker, want from the referral?

   For Angie to be safe; for Angie to live as independently as possible; to find out if Angie really is at risk.

4   In what ways do the outcomes you have identified contradict each other? How would you decide what outcomes to prioritize?

   The outcome of wanting to keep Angie safe is shared by parents and the social worker but will not necessarily be identified as clearly by Angie. This is probably not because Angie wants to place herself at risk but because she does not feel unsafe, therefore this outcome is not relevant as far as she sees things. The outcome of wanting to live as independently as possible/to live in her own community are broadly shared by the social worker and Angie. You could also argue that the outcomes of wanting to be treated as an adult and wanting Angie to listen to her parents are broadly shared, in that Angie may listen to her parents more if she feels they are treating her with the respect she feels she deserves as an adult.

   It will be easier to decide what outcomes to prioritize if you are open with Angie and her parents about this issue. For example, if you aim to achieve the outcome of helping Angie to live as independently as possible, her parents may feel that you are failing to ensure Angie listens to them and obeys their rules – this would not be accurate as you would not be trying to achieve this outcome but the potential for misunderstanding and miscommunication is self-evident.

Essentially, to decide on priority outcomes you would need to negotiate with Angie's parents and Angie, as well as ensuring you were following relevant legislation and guidance. The key message is that this must be a process of negotiation, not something you seek to impose or something you take for granted as being understood by everyone involved.

Appendix 3
Exercise 3 Known unknowns

The story we chose is about Nick Clegg's intention to 'tackle' or 'clamp down' on tax avoidance. This story was reported by the *Guardian* and the *Daily Telegraph* newspapers on 5 January 2012. You can find the original stories here: http://www.telegraph.co.uk/news/politics/nick-clegg/8993991/Nick-Clegg-vows-Budget-clampdown-on-tax-avoidance.html

and here: http://www.guardian.co.uk/politics/2012/jan/05/nick-clegg-tax-avoidance-pay

1 What did we learn about the story from the *Guardian*?

- Nick Clegg has been interviewed on the BBC's Today programme.
- Nick Clegg wants to tackle tax avoidance and excess pay.
- Nick Clegg wants the Liberal Democrats to be at the forefront of the 'battle' against excessive pay.
- Nick Clegg wants the Budget to contain measures to clamp down on tax avoidance.
- Nick Clegg argues that the approach of companies in avoiding tax angers hard-working families.
- Nick Clegg promised the next Budget would contain a general anti-avoidance rule.
- A report from the Treasury has shown a general anti-avoidance rule is feasible.
- Nick Clegg highlights the role Liberal Democrats have played in debating irresponsible capitalism.
- Nick Clegg trailed plans for greater openness and transparency in executive pay.
- Nick Clegg pointed out thousands would be lifted out of tax as a result of raising the personal allowance for income tax.
- The Liberal Democrat website revealed a YouGov poll showing 75 per cent of people who voted Liberal Democrat at the last election have deserted the party.
- Nick Clegg denied the poor were worse off because of the Coalition government's economic reforms, saying the assessment by the Institute of

> Fiscal Studies which made this suggestion was just a 'snapshot' and ignored measures such as free childcare.
> - Nick Clegg promised to lead a new debate on Europe.
> - Nick Clegg said he did not want the UK to be in a minority of one in Europe.
> - Nick Clegg said he wants to see reform of the EU and believes Europe needs a growth agenda as well as austerity.

2   What did we learn about the story from the *Daily Telegraph*?
> - Nick Clegg has been interviewed on the BBC's Today programme.
> - Nick Clegg wants to prevent abuse of the tax system.
> - David Cameron, Prime Minister, echoed his concerns.
> - Nick Clegg identified anger among ordinary people.
> - Nick Clegg reminded people that the Coalition Agreement includes a commitment to clamp down on tax avoidance and this was done at his insistence.
> - A report from the Treasury indicates a general anti-abuse rule is possible.
> - Nick Clegg highlights the achievements of the Liberal Democrats in the Coalition government, such as raising personal income tax allowance and pupil premiums.
> - Nick Clegg's overall goal is to rebalance the tax system away from work and towards unearned wealth.
> - Nick Clegg highlighted that it was the Liberal Democrats who have led the debate on bankers' bonuses, for transparency and accountability in executive pay.

3   What information has been left out?
> - The *Guardian* includes no mention of David Cameron's echoing of Nick Clegg's concerns.
> - The *Daily Telegraph* does not report the YouGov poll showing a drop in support for the Liberal Democrats.
> - The *Guardian* has an additional focus on 'excess' executive pay as well as tax avoidance; The *Daily Telegraph* has an additional focus on tax avoidance rather executive pay.
> - The *Guardian* reports the comments Nick Clegg made on Europe; The *Daily Telegraph* does not.

Neither story includes any information on who conducted the interview or what specific questions were asked. Neither story includes any response from opposition MPs. The *Guardian* story does report any response from the Institute of Fiscal Studies with regards to Nick Clegg's criticism of their report. No information is given on the suspected scale of tax avoidance in the UK and what sort of impact 'clamping down' might have.

4   Why might this be the case?

As we said in the exercise, some speculation here is necessary.

- Information was left out because of a lack of space – however, given that these stories were on the newspapers' websites, this would not seem to be a primary consideration.
- Information was left out because the journalists writing the stories did not have time to do more research.
- The *Guardian* does not report David Cameron's echoing of Nick Clegg's concerns because they supported the Liberal Democrats in the 2010 election and need to portray the Liberal Democrats as the party most concerned about tax avoidance (which also fits with the *Guardian's* overall political stance) and to downplay the Conservative party's role in this agenda.
- The *Daily Telegraph* does not report Nick Clegg's comments on excessive executive pay because they do not view any pay as excessive (which fits with their overall political stance).

Clearly, other reasons are possible and this list is not exhaustive – nevertheless, we hope this gives an indication of the variety of reasons as to why information may be included or excluded.

5   Could different information have changed the story or your view of the story?

The answer to this question must surely be 'yes'. However, here are some specific ways in which new information could have changed the story (again, some speculation is required in order to complete the exercise).

- Including the specific questions asked of Nick Clegg could have clarified why certain answers were given and given the reader an indication as to whether Nick Clegg was reporting pre-existing policy or responding to 'surprise' questions.
- Background information on the journalists writing the stories – their political affiliations, any paid roles they have had with political parties or political think-tanks and so on – could change how the story is viewed.
- Information on the effects of the achievements highlighted by Nick Clegg – for example, information on the cost of the pupil premium and any information about its success or failure could change how the story is viewed. For example, if it cost a lot of money and achieved very little, this might colour your view of the other achievements Nick Clegg mentioned.

Appendix 4
Exercise 5 Generating hypotheses

1 What is your initial, intuitive reaction? Is Robbie being abused/neglected or not (do not 'over think' this question – give the first, honest answer that comes to your mind)?

   We have deliberately not given our view on this question, as it is about your intuitive reaction, rather than ours.

2 Formulate a hypothesis that describes the information above with the conclusion that Robbie is being abused/neglected.

   Robbie is living in a high stress, low resilience household. His parents' recent separation has resulted in his mother being unable to cope, especially coming on top of Robbie's brother's diagnosis of autism. Robbie is being left to care for his brother for the majority of his time. His father was violent towards his mother and towards Robbie, hence why they separated. His father, who still visits the home, causes the bite marks and cigarette burns. His mother is unable to stop Robbie's father from visiting and may or may not be aware of the abuse. Robbie's mother may be drinking alcohol to excess to cope with the stress so Robbie has relatively easy access to alcohol in the home and a model of an adult using alcohol as a coping mechanism; this explains why Robbie has also started drinking.

3 Now formulate a hypothesis that explains the information above but with the conclusion that Robbie is not being abused/neglected.

   Robbie is living in a high stress, low reliance household. Longstanding stressors would include the high care required by Robbie's brother and a more recent stressor would be his father leaving the family home. Robbie's parents have been un-contactable because of their recent separation. Since his father left, Robbie has had to take on more caring responsibility for this brother. The bite marks have been caused by his brother but Robbie is too embarrassed to say this, hence his explanation of martial arts. As a response to this new stress, Robbie has taken up smoking but is a relative novice and hence he has burned himself. Robbie's presentation (appearing drunk) is due to prescription medication – perhaps Robbie has visited his GP and spoken about the stress and been prescribed something to help his stress or anxiety. Robbie's isolation from peers could be as a result of his changed presentation but perhaps he is also less able to visit friends and join in social activities because of his new role as carer for his brother.

4   Finally, for each hypothesis you have, think of one piece of information that, if it were true, would discount it. If you cannot think of one piece of information that would absolutely discount the hypothesis, try and think of one piece of information that would at least strongly challenge the hypothesis.

For the first hypothesis, the following information (if confirmed) would cast significant doubt on its veracity:

- *evidence that his father was not visiting the home at all, perhaps because he has emigrated;*
- *information from Robbie's brother confirming that his mother cares for him almost all of the time;*
- *evidence that Robbie is securely attached to his father (which would significantly lower the likelihood that his father is abusing him but without ruling it out conclusively);*
- *evidence of Robbie's brother being well cared for (which could lower the likelihood of his mother being too stressed to cope);*
- *evidence that Robbie is frequently out late at night with friends from outside of the school (which would cast doubt on whether Robbie's difficulties are related to his home environment as opposed to his peer environment).*

For the second hypothesis, the following information (if confirmed) would cast significant doubt on its veracity:

- *evidence from Robbie's GP that no medication has been prescribed for him;*
- *medical evidence that the bite marks are actually bite marks and not caused by a blunt instrument such as a nun-chuck;*
- *evidence suggesting that Robbie's brother has never been known to bite anyone else (which would cast doubt on whether he has bitten Robbie without ruling it out conclusively);*
- *if Robbie were unable to show you his nun-chucks (which would suggest he does not have any and has not been injuring himself with them);*
- *medical evidence that the bite marks were unlikely to have been caused by a child;*
- *evidence from other professionals that they have been able to contact Robbie's mother relatively easily (which could suggest she has been avoiding calls from the school in particular);*
- *information from Robbie's brother confirming that his mother cares for him almost all of the time;*
- *evidence that Robbie is disorganized in his attachment relationship with either his mother or father (which would significantly increase the likelihood of abuse but without confirming it definitively).*

Appendix 5
Exercise 7 Empathic responses

In practice, many practitioners respond in one of these two ways (with each one representing a typical response from the Forrester et al. study):

1   This is contradictory to what the school is saying; the school feel you have presented drunk and this is why we've got the referral and we're concerned. If you're saying it's the anti-depressants, you need to go back to your GP and adjust the dose as it's clearly a problem.
2   Can I see the bottle of anti-depressants? Where does it say that on the label?

As Shemmings (2011) notes, the problem with both of these is that they are implicitly assuming the parent is lying. Some practitioners will no doubt feel that the parent is lying and indeed, this is possible. However, as a *first response* to what the parent has told you, either of these responses could almost have been designed to shut down any further discussion and to ensure the parent does not build up any trust or expectation that you want to listen to them. The power of empathic responses is that they open up discussions, prompt more information sharing and, ultimately, make it easier to assess the risk or need in any given situation.

Examples of empathic responses:

1   That sounds terrible for you (actually a sympathetic rather than empathetic response but still better than the above two options).
2   You feel angry because you feel the school have accused you of something that is not true (by adding 'you feel', the worker is ensuring that are not agreeing with the parent).
3   You must feel as if you are in a very difficult position, given what the school have said and now having me visit you at home.
4   So you're finding it so stressful being a mum at present that you have felt that you need to talk to your GP about it. Can you tell me more about your stress?

This is not an exhaustive list of empathic responses but the principles underlying them (apart from the first, which is sympathetic not empathetic) is that you are indicating the person talking to you has been heard and understood but more than this, that you have noted their emotional reaction and suggested a reason for it or confirmed that you have understood their reasoning for it.

Appendix 6
Exercise 8 Keep it simple

Task: Re-write the following two paragraphs, aiming for (1) clarity and (2) brevity (you should feel free to speculate as required in order to re-write the paragraphs more clearly).

(1) I visited Mr Cooke at home and interviewed him about his daily life. Mr Cooke informed me that he feels his self-care skills are reasonably good; Mr Cooke feels he is able to meet his own needs for nutrition, for personal care and for stimulation at home. In terms of social relationships, Mr Cooke is part of various networks including a local mosque. However, I had the impression from interviewing Mr Cooke that he showed some evidence of short-term memory loss and this was non-commensurate for a man of his age. On observation, the home environment was reasonably clean and tidy – however, I did note several areas of concern, including a poorly maintained aquarium. With his consent, I spoke with Mr Cooke's GP who informed me that he regularly visits Mr Cooke at home and finds him to be often confused and disoriented.

I visited Mr Cooke at home and we talked about the things he does day to day. Mr Cooke told me that he is able to make himself a cup of tea, that he can wash and take a bath without help and that he likes to read, listen to the radio and watch TV, all of which he told me he can do without help. Mr Cooke attends mosque every Friday and he often talks to the other people who attend at the same time. However, I did notice during the visit that Mr Cooke told me things more than once and several times he asked to be reminded who I was. This suggested to me that he has some short-term memory loss and that he was more forgetful than most other men of his age, in my experience. The house was clean and tidy apart from a fish tank, which was quite cloudy and murky.

(2) Mrs Shah has been admitted to her local mental health hospital following an attempted suicide. Mrs Shah is in the hospital via a voluntary admission. Mrs Shah has presented with some depressive behaviour on the ward. Mrs Shah often makes statements that could be considered examples of suicidal ideation. Mrs Shah informs that she does not feel her life is worth living. While on the ward, I am aware that Mrs Shah has been visited by members of her extended family network, namely her nephew. These visits seem to have a positive impact on Mrs Shah's self-esteem and her presentation in periods shortly after these visits is also improved. Mrs Shah likely requires an extended in-patient admission if her risk profile in future is to be improved.

Mrs Shah is currently in hospital following an event in which she took an overdose of sleeping pills. Mrs Shah has chosen to stay in hospital for the time being. Mrs Shah has at times appeared very sad on the ward and has found it hard to get out of bed; Mrs Shah has also not been eating very much – these could be signs of depression. Mrs Shah has told me how she thinks her family would be better off if she were dead and talked about how she feels she has very little positive in her life to live for. Mrs Shah's nephew has visited her on the ward and it is noticeable that after these visits, Mrs Shah appears happier for a short while – she smiles more and may have something to eat. Mrs Shah will also put her make-up on if she knows her nephew is going to visit. I would worry about Mrs Shah if she were to go home at the moment as I do not know enough about her life at home and whether she might try to take her own life again.

Appendix 7
Exercise 9 Reflection in practice

This is one possible way of completing this exercise.

1 How would you describe 'what' is happening in the case study above? What are your initial 'gut' or intuitive feelings about what is going on?

   Joan has reported she cannot continue to care for her mother, Mrs Bee, at home. Mrs Bee appears to be living relatively independently although she did exhibit some repetition and vagueness in her stories. Joan and Mrs Bee do not appear to get on very well.

2 Once you are clear on the 'what', can you now say 'so what'? In other words, given what you think is going on, what is the significance of it?

   Regardless of whether Mrs Bee can or cannot continue to live relatively independently, Joan may decide she cannot continue supporting her and this will be significant for the family. There is also likely to be significance in the 'cool' relationship between Mrs Bee and Joan. It could also be significant that Mrs Bee did show some evidence of repetition and vagueness – this could indicate a more serious impairment.

3 What would you do next? What do you think Joan and Mrs Bee might do next?

   Based on this 'what' and 'so what', it would be important to explore exactly what support Joan is offering to Mrs Bee and how significant the potential withdrawal of it would be. Further exploration of the relationship between Mrs Bee and Joan could also suggest reasons as to why Joan feels Mrs Bee cannot live independently and needs to move to a residential home. Getting to know Mrs Bee better could also help suggest potential reasons for her vagueness and repetitiveness and would also help you understand whether this is her 'baseline' presentation or whether she has just having an 'off day'.

Appendix 8
Exercise 11 Applying tools for critical analysis

Task 1 Based on what you know so far, complete a cultural review of the family.
We have not included a cultural review as these are personal for each practitioner. In other words, different practitioners will have different information, biases and sources of information about different cultures. For example, a cultural review completed by a practitioner from the same cultural background as Mrs Bee would likely be significantly different from a cultural review completed by either of us (who are not from the same cultural background as Mrs Bee).

Task 2 Based on what you know so far, complete a decision tree for Mrs Bee.

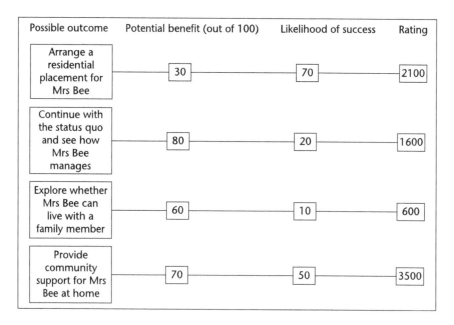

Possible outcome	Potential benefit (out of 100)	Likelihood of success	Rating
Arrange a residential placement for Mrs Bee	30	70	2100
Continue with the status quo and see how Mrs Bee manages	80	20	1600
Explore whether Mrs Bee can live with a family member	60	10	600
Provide community support for Mrs Bee at home	70	50	3500

As you do so, ask yourself the following questions:

a) How have I decided what the options are that should be included in the decision tree? What options have I excluded and what is my basis for excluding them?

We have taken the four most obvious possible outcomes and used those. We admit to lacking a great deal of creativity in our answer or to really exploring what community support might look like. If we were minded to consider community support, we would want to complete another decision tree based on what a range of different community support options. Equally, we would do the same if we were minded to consider a family placement – e.g. we would want to complete another decision tree based on the individual options within the family.

b) On what basis have I selected the numbers to insert in the 'potential benefit' and 'likelihood' columns? What might persuade me to change the numbers? Have I massaged the figures to suit my preferred figures? How could I defend against the possibility that I have?

When considering the potential benefits, we have done so from the viewpoint of direct benefits (such as whether Mrs Bee would be happy in a residential home) and peripheral benefits (such as the impact it might have on the family relationships and dynamics). For example, when considering the issue of a residential placement, we have placed it at higher than zero because it might ease the tension in the relationship between Mrs Bee and Joan, which would likely be a peripheral benefit in our view.

In the likelihood column, we have also tried to include some reference to how the wider family would respond. For example, when considering maintaining the status quo, we tried to take into account Joan's imagined response to this, which we think would be to continue trying to persuade professionals that her mother is not safe at home, which would then have a disruptive affect on this outcome. Similarly, when considering a family placement, we have tried to take into account the likely response of Mrs Bee's children to such a suggestion, rather than simply imagining that they will be fully behind this outcome. We imagine that both Joan and Peter would oppose this idea, albeit for differing reasons.

c) How might a decision tree completed by Mrs Bee, Peter or Joan look? What is the significance of any differences that might exist between their decision trees and mine?

We have not included examples of what a decision tree might look like purely from Mrs Bee's or other family members' perspectives – we are confident you will be able to do this, especially having seen our example above.

Task 3 Based on what you know so far, complete a needs analysis of Mrs Bee.

	Needs	Outcomes
Health	Mrs Bee may have deteriorating memory, the cause of which is unclear	To identify if Mrs Bee's memory loss is age-related or related to any other factor, such as an illness
Family and social relationships	Mrs Bee needs to see her children regularly	For Mrs Bee to see at least one of her children at least once a fortnight
	Mrs Bee has a friend who she needs to visit occasionally	For Mrs Bee to see her friend at least once a month
Identity	Mrs Bee sees herself as an independent and capable adult	For Mrs Bee to be able to do the things that contribute to the view she has of herself as independent and capable *(this would need further exploration – for example, is being able to visit her friend part of this or is it doing her own shopping, doing her own cooking, etc.?)*
Ensuring safety	Mrs Bee needs to be safe when she goes out into the local community, to visit her friend or for any other reasons	For Mrs Bee to manage to go out and come home regularly without having to notify the police so that they can find her

N.B. We have selected just four dimensions for this needs analysis – in practice, you would be expected to look much more widely at Mrs Bee's needs or indeed the needs of the whole family.

   a)   How does the needs analysis help with your decision-making about Mrs Bee?
       Potentially, in several ways. It could open up a discussion with Mrs Bee about residential care and what makes her so strongly opposed to it. It might be that Mrs Bee fears she would lose her identity and her social relationships – if so, a needs analysis that clearly laid this out could help reassure Mrs Bee that social calls and independent activity could be part of her care plan, regardless of whether she lived at home or elsewhere. In our example, the fact that we are unsure what contributes to Mrs Bee's view that she is an independent and capable adult would prompt us to want to explore this further with Mrs Bee, to find out what aspects of her life fulfil this identity for her.

   b)   Does the needs analysis and clear identification of the outcomes change the decision tree you completed previously? If so, how? If not, why not?
       It would help us develop a further decision tree – for example, if we wanted to expand the outcome of Mrs Bee living at home with community support, being clear about where and how she did need assistance would help us develop a clearer idea

about what community support was actually needed. Our view is that this example shows neatly how tools such as a needs analysis and a decision tree can be combined together, both providing feedback for the other and improving our overall analysis of the situation.

Notes

Introduction

1   For children, Serious Case Reviews should be undertaken in England and Wales whenever a child dies and abuse and neglect is suspected or known to be a factor (as well as in cases of suspected suicide). Serious Case Reviews can also be held when a child has been seriously harmed through neglect or abuse, when a parent has been murdered or following a violent assault by another child or adult *and* there are concerns arising from the case regarding inter-agency working by safeguarding agencies (see Chapter 8, *Working Together to Safeguard Children,* Department for Children, Schools and Families 2010). For adults, it is recommended that Serious Case Reviews should be undertaken whenever an adult dies in combination with suspected or actual abuse or neglect or when an adult experiences a potentially life-threatening injury through possible abuse or neglect *and* there are concerns arising from the case regarding inter-agency working by safeguarding agencies (Association of Directors of Adult Social Services 2006).

Chapter 2

1   Protection Of Vulnerable Adults, Initial Child Protection Conference, telephone call (often used as a short-hand in recordings), Resource Allocation Panel, Emotional and Behavioural Difficulties and Assistant Director respectively.

References

Ajzen, I. (1991) The theory of planned behavior. *Organizational Behavior and Human Decision Processes,* 50: 179–211.

Association of Directors of Adult Social Services (2006) *Vulnerable Adult Serious Case Review Guidance: Developing a Local Protocol.* London: ADASS.

Barrett, T.R. and Etheridge, J.B. (1992) Verbal hallucinations in normals, I: people who hear 'voices'. *Applied Cognitive Psychology,* 6: 379–87.

Beck, U. (1992) *Risk Society: Towards a New Modernity.* London: Sage Publications.

Beddoe, L. (2011) Investing in the future: social workers talk about research. *British Journal of Social Work,* 41: 557–75.

Benner, P. and Tanner, C. (1987) Clinical judgment: how expert nurses use intuition. *American Journal of Nursing,* 87: 23–31.

Bogo, M. and McKnight, K. (2006) Clinical supervision in social work: a review of the research literature. *The Clinical Supervisor,* 24(1–2): 49–67.

Brandon, M., Belderson, P., Warren, C. et al. (2008) *Analysing Child Deaths and Serious Injury through Abuse and Neglect: What can we learn? A Biennial Analysis of Serious Case Reviews 2003–2005.* London: Department for Children, Schools and Families.

Brandon, M., Bailey, S., Belderson, P. et al. (2009) *Understanding Serious Case Reviews and their Impact: A Biennial Analysis of Serious Case Reviews 2005–07.* London: Department for Children, Schools and Families.

Braunstein-Bercovitz, H., Dimentman-Ashkenazi, I. and Lubow, R.E. (2001) Stress affects the selection of relevant from irrelevant stimuli. *Emotion Washington DC,* 1(2): 182–92.

British Association of Social Workers (2011) *Research on Supervision in Social Work.* http://cdn. basw.co.uk/upload/basw_13955-1.pdf (accessed 6 June 2012).

Broadhurst, K., Wastell, D., White, S. et al. (2010) Performing 'initial assessment': identifying the latent conditions for error at the front-door of local authority children's service. *British Journal of Social Work,* 40(2): 352–70.

Brookfield, S. (2009) The concept of critical reflection: promises and contradictions. *European Journal of Social Work,* 12(3): 293–304.

Burton, S. (2009) *The Oversight and Review of Cases in the Light of Changing Circumstances and New Information: How do People Respond to New (and Challenging) Information?* London: National Children's Bureau.

Carson, E., King, S. and Papatraianou, L.H. (2011) Resilience among social workers: the role of informal learning in the workplace. *Practice: Social Work in Action,* 5: 267–78.

Children's Workforce Development Council and Skills for Care (2007) *Providing Effective Supervision: A Workforce Development Tool.* London: CWDW and Skills for Care.

Cioffi, J. (1997) Heuristics, servants to intuition, in clinical decision making. *Journal of Advanced Nursing,* 26: 203–8.

Cleaver, H. and Walker, S. (2004) From policy to practice: the implementation of a new framework for social work assessments of children and families. *Child and Family Social Work*, 9: 81–90.

Collins, E. and Daly, E. (2011) *Decision Making and Social Work in Scotland: The Role of Evidence and Practice Wisdom*. Glasgow: The Institute for Research and Innovation in Social Services.

Community Care (2011) *Cultural Misunderstandings Contributed to Baby's Death*. http://www.communitycare.co.uk/Articles/13/10/2011/117602/social-workers-misread-ghanaian-culture-in-baby-death-case.htm (accessed 28 May 2012).

Covey, S. (2005) *The 7 Habits of Highly Effective People*. New York: Simon and Schuster.

Croskerry, P. (2009) Diagnostic reasoning: a universal model of diagnostic reasoning. *Academic Medicine*, 84: 1022–8.

Dalzell, R. and Saywer, E. (2011) *Putting Analysis into Assessment: Undertaking Assessments of Need – A Toolkit for Practitioners* (2nd revised edition). London: National Children's Bureau.

Damasio, A. (1991) *Somatic Markers and the Guidance of Behavior*. New York: Oxford University Press.

Damasio, A. (1994) *Descartes' Error: Emotion, Reason, and the Human Brain*. New York: Grosset/Putnam.

Dane, E., Baer, M., Pratt, M. and Oldham, G. (2011) Rational versus intuitive problem solving: how thinking 'off the beaten path' can stimulate creativity. *Psychology of Aesthetics, Creativity, and the Arts*, 5: 3–12.

Danziger, S., Levav, J. and Avnaim-Pesso, L. (2011) Extraneous factors in judicial decisions. *Proceedings of the National Academy of Sciences of the United States of America*. DOI: 10.1073/pnas.1018033108

Dawkins, R. (1998) Postmodernism disrobed. *Nature*, 394: 141–3.

Department for Children, Schools and Families (2010) *Working Together to Safeguard Children: A Guide to Inter-agency Working to Safeguard and Promote the Welfare of Children*. London: TSO.

Department for Constitutional Affairs (2005) *The Mental Capacity Act 2005*. London: Office of Public Sector Information.

Department of Health, Department for Education and Employment and Home Office (2000) *Framework for the Assessment of Children in Need and their Families*. London: TSO.

Dijksterhuis, A. (2004) Think different: the merits of unconscious thought in preference development and decision making. *Journal of Personality and Social Psychology*, 87: 586–98.

Ellis, K. (2004) Promoting rights or avoiding litigation: the introduction of the 1998 Human Rights Act into adult social care in England. *European Journal of Social Work*, 7(3): 321–40.

Escher, S., Romme, M., Buiks, A., Delespaul, P. and van Os, J. (2002) Formation of delusional ideation in adolescents hearing voices: a prospective study. *American Journal of Medical Genetics*, 114: 913–20.

Eysenck, H.J. (1960) Classification and the problems of diagnosis. In H.J. Eysenck (ed.) *Handbook of Abnormal Psychology*. London: Pitman, pp. 1–31.

Fonagy, P., Steele, M., Steele, H., Moran, G. and Higgitt, A. (1991) The capacity for under-standing mental states: the reflective self in parent and child and its significance for security of attachment. *Infant Mental Health Journal*, 12: 201–18.

Fonagy, P. and Target, M. (2001) War and attachment: a theoretical perspective. *Young Minds Magazine*, 55(November/December): 26–7.

Forder, A. (1976) *Concepts in Social Administration: A Framework for Analysis*. London: Routledge.

Forrester, D., McCambridge, J., Waissbein, C. and Rollcink, S. (2008) Communication skills in child protection: how do social workers talk to parents? *Child & Family Social Work*, 13: 41–51.

Fosha, D. (2003) Dyadic regulation and experiential work with emotion and relatedness in trauma and disorganised attachment. In M. Solomon and D. Siegal (eds) *Healing Trauma, Attachment, Mind, Body and Brain*. London: Norton and Co.

Frederick, S. (2005) Cognitive reflection and decision making. *Journal of Economic Perspectives*, 19: 25–42.

Gailliot, M.T., Baumeister, R.F., DeWall, C.N. et al. (2007) Self-control relies on glucose as a limited energy source: willpower is more than a metaphor. *Journal of Personality and Social Psychology*, 92: 325–36.

Ghazinoory, S., Abdi, M. and Azadegan-Mehr, M. (2011) SWOT methodology: a state-of-the-art review for the past, a framework for the future. *Journal of Business Economics & Management,* 12(1): 24–48.

Gibbs, G. (1988) *Learning by Doing: A Guide to Teaching and Learning Methods*. Oxford: Further Education Unit, Oxford Polytechnic.

Gordon, J., Cooper, B. and Dumbleton, S. (2009) *How Do Social Workers Use Evidence in Practice?* Maidenhead: Open University Press.

Gould, N. and Baldwin, M. (eds) (2004) *Social Work, Critical Reflection and the Learning Organisation*. Aldershot: Ashgate.

Greene, J. (2007) Why are VMPFC patients more utilitarian? A dual-process theory of moral judgment explains? *Trends in Cognitive Sciences*, 11: 322–3.

Guardian (2011) *Nurse jailed for killing her baby by force-feeding*. http://www.guardian.co.uk/uk/2011/nov/11/nurse-jailed-baby-force-feeding (accessed 28 May 2012).

Haidt, J. (2007) *The Happiness Hypothesis: Putting Ancient Wisdom to the Test of Modern Science*. London: Arrow.

Hammond, K., Hamm, R., Grassia, J. and Pearson, T. (1997) Direct comparison of the efficacy of intuitive and analytical cognition in expert judgement. In W. Goldstein and R. Hogarth (eds) *Research on Judgement and Decision Making: Currents, Connections and Controversies*. Cambridge: Cambridge University Press.

Harkness, D. and Hensley, H. (1991) Changing the focus of social work supervision: effects on client satisfaction and generalized contentment. *Journal of Social Work*, 36: 506–12.

Heath, C. and Heath, D. (2011) *Switch: How to Change Things when Change is Hard*. London: Random House Business.

Helm, D. (2009) *Analysis and Getting it Right for Every Child: A Discussion Paper*. http://www.scotland.gov.uk/Resource/0038/00385953.pdf (accessed 6 June 2012).

Helm, D. (2011) Judgements or assumptions? The role of analysis in assessing children and young people's needs. *British Journal of Social Work Practice*, 41: 894–911.

Howe, D. (2008) *The Emotionally Intelligent Social Worker*. Basingstoke: Palgrave Macmillan.

Howe, D., Brandon, M., Hinings, D. and Schofield, G. (1999) *Attachment Theory, Child Maltreatment and Family Support: A Practice and Assessment Model*. London: Macmillan Press Ltd.

Hudson, C.G. (2000) From social Darwinism to self-organization: implications for social change theory. *Social Service Review*, 74: 533–59.

Janis, I. and Mann, L. (1976) Coping with decisional conflict: an analysis of how stress affects decision-making suggests intervention to improve the process. *American Scientist*, 64: 657–67.

Kadushin, A. and Harkness, D. (2002) *Supervision in Social Work,* 4th edn, New York: Columbia University Press.

Kahneman, D. (2011) *Thinking Fast and Slow*. London: Allen Lane.

Kemshall, H. (2002) *Risk, Social Policy and Welfare*. Buckingham: Open University Press.

Kemshall, H., Parton, N., Walsh, M. and Waterson, J. (1997) Concepts of risk in relation to organizational structure and functioning within the personal social services and probation. *Social Policy and Administration*, 31(3): 213–32.

Keys, M. (2009a) Determining the skills for child protection practice: from quandary to quagmire? *Child Abuse Review*. 18: 297–315.

Keys, M. (2009b) Determining the skills for child protection practice: emerging from the quagmire! *Child Abuse Review*. 18: 316–32.

Klas, L. and Hawkins, F. (1997) Time management as a stressor for helping professionals: implications for employment. *Journal of Employment Counselling*, 34: 2–6.

Klein, G. (1999) *Sources of Power: How People Make Decisions*. Cambridge, MA: MIT Press.

Laing, R. (1990) *The Divided Self: An Existential Study of Sanity and Madness*. London: Penguin.

Laming, L. (2003) *The Victoria Climbié Inquiry*. London: TSO.

Laming, L. (2009) *The Protection of Children in England: A Progress Report*. London: TSO.

Lamond, D. and Thompson, C. (2000) Intuition and analysis in decision making and choice. *Journal of Nursing Scholarship*, 32: 411–14.

LeDoux, J. (1996) *The Emotional Brain: The Mysterious Underpinnings of Emotional Life*. New York: Simon & Schuster.

Luna, D. and Gupta, S. (2001) An integrative framework for cross-cultural consumer behavior. *International Marketing Review*, 18: 45–69.

Lynch, M. and Cicchetti, D. (1998) An ecological-transactional analysis of children and contexts: the longitudinal interplay among child maltreatment, community violence, and children's symptomatology. *Development and Psychopathology*, 10: 235–57.

McCracken, G. (1988) *Culture and Consumption: New Approaches to the Symbolic Character of Consumer Goods and Activities*. Bloomington, IN: Indiana University Press.

McEwan, B. and Sapolsky, R. (1995) Stress and cognitive function. *Current Opinion in Neurobiology*, 5: 205–16.

MacKenzie, M.J., Kotch, J.B., Lee, L.C., Augsberger, A. and Hutto, N. (2011) The cumulative ecological risk model of child maltreatment and child behavioral outcomes: reconceptualizing reported maltreatment as risk factor. *Children & Youth Services Review*, 33: 2392–8.

Mäntysaari, M. (2005) Realism as a foundation for social work knowledge. *Qualitative Social Work*. 4(1): 87–98.

Mitchell, F., Lunt, N. and Shaw, I. (2009) *Practitioner Research in Social Services: A Literature Review (summary)*. Dundee: Institute for Research and Innovation in Social Services.

Moll, J. and de Oliveira-Souza, R. (2007) Response to Greene: moral sentiments and reason: friends or foe? *Trends in Cognitive Sciences*, 11: 323–4.

Morrison, T. (2007) Emotional intelligence, emotion and social work: context, characteristics, complications and contribution. *British Journal of Social Work*, 37: 245–63.

Munro, E. (1996) Avoidable and unavoidable mistakes in child protection work. *British Journal of Social Work*, 26: 793–808.

Munro, E. (1999) Common errors of reasoning in child protection work. *Child Abuse and Neglect*, 23: 745–58. http://eprints.lse.ac.uk/358/ (accessed June 2012).

Munro, E. (2002) Integrating intuition and analysis in child protection. *Social Welfare at Berkeley*, Fall: 7–9.

Munro, E. (2005) A systems approach to investigating child abuse deaths. *British Journal of Social Work*, 35: 531–46.

Munro, E. (2008) *Effective Child Protection Practice*. London: Sage Publications.

Munro, E. (2009) Guide to analytic and intuitive reasoning. *Community Care Inform* [online] http://www.ccinform.co.uk/Articles/2009/08/20/3390/Guide+to+analytic+and+intuitive+reasoning.html (accessed June 2012).

Munro, E. (2010) *The Munro Review of Child Protection. Part One: A Systems Analysis*. London: TSO.

Munro, E. (2011a) *The Munro Review of Child Protection. Interim Report: The Childs Journey*. London: TSO.

Munro, E. (2011b) *The Munro Review of Child Protection. Final Report: A Child-centred System*. London: TSO.

Munro, E. and Hubbard, A. (2011) A systems approach to evaluating organisational change in children's social care. *British Journal of Social Work*, 41(4): 726–43.

Nicolas, J. (2012) *Conducting the Home Visit in Child Protection*. Maidenhead: Open University Press.

Norenzayan, A., Smith, E.E., Kim, B. and Nisbett, R.E. (2002) Cultural preferences for formal versus intuitive reasoning. *Cognitive Science*, 26: 653–84.

Orme, J. and Shemmings, D. (2010) *Developing Research Based Social Work Practice*. Basingstoke: Palgrave Macmillan.

Parton, N. (1998) Reconfiguring child welfare practices: risk, advanced liberalism, and the government of freedom. In A. Chambon, A. Irving and L. Epstein (eds) *Reading Foucault for Social Work*. New York: Columbia University Press, pp. 103–30.

Pawson, R., Boaz, A., Grayson, L., Long, A. and Barnes, C. (2003) *Types and Quality of Knowledge in Social Care*. London: Social Care Institute for Excellence.

Payne, M. (2002) *Modern Social Work Theory*. Chicago: Lyceum Books.

Pearce, C. (2007) Ten steps to carrying out a SWOT analysis. *Nursing Management*, 14: 25.

Pennebaker, J. and Seagal, J. (1999) Forming a story: the health benefits of narrative. *Journal of Clinical Pyschology*, 55: 1243–54.

Pennington, N. and Hastie, R. (1991) A cognitive theory of juror decision making: the story model. *Cordoza Law Review*, 13: 519–57.

Pincus, A. and Minahan, A. (1973) *Social Work Practice: Model and Method*. Illinois: F. E. Peacock Publishers, Inc.

Pithouse, A. (1998) *Social Work: The Social Organisation of an Invisible Trade*, 2nd edn. Aldershot: Ashgate.

Platt, D. (2011) Assessments of children and families: learning and teaching the skills of analysis. *Social Work Education*, 30: 157–69.

Pretz, J.E. (2008) Intuition versus analysis: strategy and experience in complex everyday problem solving. *Memory and Cognition*, 36(3): 554–66.

Professional Social Work (2012) *Survey confirms worst fears about social work caseloads and morale*. British Association of Social Work.

Reder, P. and Duncan, S. (1999) *Lost Innocents: A Follow-up Study of Fatal Child Abuse*. London: Routledge.

Rew, L. and Barron, E. (1987) Intuition: a neglected hallmark of nursing knowledge. *Advances in Nursing Science*, 10: 49–62.

Rolfe, G., Freshwater, D. and Jasper, M. (eds) (2001) *Critical Reflection for Nursing and the Helping Professions*. Basingstoke: Palgrave.

Rowlings, C. (1995) Supervision and work with older people. In J. Pritchard (ed) *Good Practice in Supervision*. London: Jessica Kingsley Press, pp. 71–84.

Ruch, G. (2005) Relationship-based practice and reflective practice: holistic approaches to contemporary child care social work. *Child & Family Social Work*, 10(2): 111–23.

Ruch, G., Turney, D. and Ward, A. (2010) *Relationship-based Social Work: Getting to the Heart of Practice*. London: Jessica Kingsley Press.

Seden, J. (2001) Assessment of children in need and their families: a literature review. In Department of Health, *Studies Informing the Framework for the Assessment of Children in Need and their Families*. London: The Stationery Office.

Selart, M., Tvedt Johansen, S., Holmesland, T. and Grønhaug, K. (2008) Can intuitive and analytical decision styles explain managers' evaluation of information technology? *Management Decision*, 46: 1326–41.

Shemmings, D. (2011) What social workers need to know about empathy. *Community Care*. http://www.communitycare.co.uk/Articles/31/10/2011/117682/empathy-and-neuroscience-powerful-tools-for-social-workers.htm) (accessed 12 November 2012).

Shemmings, D. and Reeves, J. (2012) *'Rosie' and 'Rosie 2' Serious Training Games*, The Centre for Child Protection, University of Kent. www.kent.ac.uk/sspssr/ccp/game.index.html (accessed 15 January 2013).

Shier, M.L. and Graham, J.R. (2011) Work-related factors that impact social work practitioners' subjective well-being: well-being in the workplace. *Journal of Social Work*, 11(4): 402–21.

Simon, H. (1957) *Models of Man: Social and Rational*. New York: John Wiley and Sons, Inc.

Sjöberg, L. (2003) Intuitive vs. analytical decision making: which is preferred? *Scandinavian Journal of Management*, 19: 17–29.

Sloman, S.A. (1996) The empirical case for two systems of reasoning. *Psychological Bulletin*, 119: 3–22.

Social Work Inspection Agency (2010) *Improving Social Work in Scotland*. Edinburgh: Social Work Inspection Agency.

Social Work Reform Board (2009) *Building a Safe, Confident Future: The Final Report of the Social Work Task Force*. London: TSO.

Solomon, S. (2002) *How Jurors Make Decisions: A Practical and Systematic Approach to Understanding Juror Behaviour*. New York: DOAR.

Stewart, S., Lam, T., Betson, C., Wong, C. and Wong, A. (1999) A prospective analysis of stress and academic performance in the first two years of medical school. *Medical Education*, 33: 243–50.

Tammet, D. (2007) *Born on a Blue Day*. London: Hodder Paperbacks.

Tew, J. (2005) *Social Perspectives in Mental Health: Developing Social Models to Understand and Work With Mental Distress*. London: Jessica Kingsley.

Tameside Adult Safeguarding Partnership (2011) *Executive Summary for the Serious Case Review in Respect of Adult A*. http://www.tameside.gov.uk/socialcare/adultabuse/seriouscasereview (accessed 15 January 2013).

Tsui, Ming-sum (2005) *Social Work Supervision: Context and Concepts*. Thousand Oaks, CA, London, New Delhi: Sage.

Turney, D. (2009) *Analysis and Critical Thinking in Assessment*. Dartington: Research in Practice.

Turney, D., Platt, D., Selwyn, J. and Farmer, E. (2011) *Social Work Assessment of Children in Need: What Do We Know? Messages From Research*. Bristol: University of Bristol.

Walker, J. (2008) Communication and social work from an attachment perspective. *Journal of Social Work Practice*, 22: 5–13.

Warner, J. and Sharland, E. (2010) Editorial. *British Journal of Social Work*, 40(4): 1035–45.

Webb, S.A. (2006) *Social Work in a Risk Society: Social and Political Perspectives*. Basingstoke: Palgrave Macmillan.

Wenner, D. and Cusimano, G. (2000) Combating juror bias, *Trial Magazine*, June, p. 30.

Westhues, A., LaFrance, J. and Schmidt, G. (2001) A SWOT analysis of social work education in Canada. *Social Work Education*, 20: 35–56.

White, S. (2009) Fabled uncertainty in social work. *Journal of Social Work*, 9: 222–35.

White, S., Hall, C. and Peckover, S. (2008) The descriptive tyranny of the common assessment framework: technologies of categorization and professional practice in child welfare. *British Journal of Social Work*, 39: 1197–217.

Wilkins, D. (2010) I'm not sure what I want (and I don't know how to get it): how do social care workers perceive the parental relationships of children with autistic spectrum conditions? *Journal of Social Work Practice*, 24: 89–101.

Wilkins, D. (2011) Specific caregiver behaviour. In D. Shemmings and Y. Shemmings (eds) *Understanding Disorganised Attachment*. London: Jessica Kingsley Publishers.

Wilkins, D. (2012) Ethical dilemmas in social work practice: young adults with autism. *Journal of Ethics and Social Welfare*, 16(2): 127–33.

Williams, A. and McCann, J. (2006) *Care Planning for Looked After Children: A Toolkit for Practitioners*. London: NCB.

Wilson, T. (2011) *Redirect: The Surprising New Science of Psychological Change*. London: Allen Lane.

Zeira, A. and Rosen, A. (2000) Unraveling 'tacit knowledge': what social workers do and why they do it. *Social Service Review*, 74: 103–23.

Index

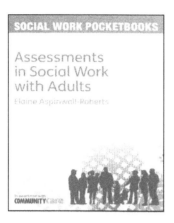

ASSESSMENTS IN SOCIAL WORK WITH ADULTS

Elaine Aspinwall-Roberts

9780335245215 (Paperback)
May 2012

eBook also available

This accessible survival guide shows social workers how to make their assessments the best, most effective and person-centred they can be.

Part of a new Social Work Pocketbooks series, the book is friendly, non-patronising and realistic about the day-to-day difficulties and challenges associated with assessing adults. It encourages you to reflect on how you work, and what you bring to the task.

Key features:

- Practical examples, advice and tips, including dealing with pitfalls
- Good practice and point of law reminders
- Fresh ideas on how to develop your assessment skills with adults

www.openup.co.uk

CONDUCTING THE HOME VISIT
IN CHILD PROTECTION

Joanna Nicolas

9780335245277 (Paperback)
May 2012

eBook also available

Conducting a home visit is a fundamental part of a social worker's role, but in practical terms many key issues are overlooked during social work training.

Part of a new Social Work Pocketbooks series, this is a practical guide to conducting home visits, a task which many feel unprepared for and is fraught with difficulties.

Key features:

- Real case examples
- Realistic solutions to the everyday difficulties you face
- Examples of what to say

www.openup.co.uk

 OPEN UNIVERSITY PRESS
McGraw - Hill Education

SUPERVISION

Bill McKitterick

9780335245253 (Paperback)
October 2012

eBook also available

Supervision has a special place in the development of social work practice skills and continuing professional development. However it can be neglected or overshadowed. Part of a new **Social Work Pocketbooks** series, this book focuses on the practical and workable ways for preparing for and using supervision, ensuring it is provided and making improvements if it is not working for you.

Key features:

- Practical ways for both the supervisor and social worker to prepare for and use supervision
- Strategies to improve supervision or get it started again when it has fallen into disuse
- Realistic examples of good and bad practice

www.openup.co.uk

OPEN UNIVERSITY PRESS
McGraw - Hill Education

TEAMWORKING SKILLS FOR SOCIAL WORKERS

Ruben Martin

9780335246052 (Paperback)
June 2013

eBook also available

Social workers are not completely autonomous professionals working alone. They are members of teams and need to work in collaboration with colleagues and other professionals in order to practice effectively.

This book provides a practical and applied overview of the different types of teams social workers will encounter, and explores the dynamics present when people work together, the roles individuals play and the skills necessary for effective teamworking in the context of social work practice.

Key features:

- Checklists to help the reader rate their capability and plan ways of developing skills for which they score low
- Reflection points
- Activities

www.openup.co.uk